The AI Policy Sourcebook 2019

MARC ROTENBERG

Electronic Privacy Information Center
WASHINGTON DC

Electronic Privacy Information Center
1718 Connecticut Ave. NW
Suite 200
Washington, DC 20009

Visit the EPIC Bookstore
http://www.epic.org/bookstore/

Edition 2019
Printed in the United States of America
All Rights Reserved

ISBN-13: 978-1-7326139-2-8
ISBN-10: 1-7326139-2-3

Table of Contents

Corporate AI Guidelines

AI Resources

INTRODUCTION

For over two decades, the Electronic Privacy Information Center has published the *Privacy Law Sourcebook* with the goal of providing to policymakers, researchers, journalists and the general public an essential compendium of privacy law and resources. PLS has featured the complete texts of national laws and international agreements, as well as useful resources, publications, and organizations. We have also made some effort, with each publication, to identify key developments and recent trends. Over time, PLS has provided a series of snapshots on the state of privacy around the world.

We are undertaking a similar project for AI with the first edition of the EPIC *AI Policy Sourcebook*. AI has long been of interest to computers scientists, ethicists, and, of course, science fiction writers. But now AI has emerged as a top priority for policy makers. Earlier this year German Chancellor Angela Merkel urged the creation of a comprehensive legal framework for AI, comparable to the GDPR, the data protection regime of the European Union. Incoming President of the European Commission Ursula von der Leyen has proposed action on AI policy in the first 100 days of the new Commission.

Professional and technical societies, including the ACM and the IEEE, have been on the front lines of AI policy from the start, focusing specifically on the social consequences and professional responsibility associated with the development of AI systems. Private companies have also announced significant policy frameworks for AI, which seek to address growing public concern. And Isaac Asimov's Three Laws of Robotics continue to ground many discussions about a world of intelligent devices.

Perhaps the two most significant developments in the AI policy field over the past years were the OECD AI Principles and the Universal Guidelines for AI. The OECD AI Principles are the first government-endorsed framework AI policy, the beginning of national law and international agreements for the regulation of AI. The OECD Principles were endorsed by 42 governments this year and also by the G-20, meeting in Osaka. Also of significance are the Universal Guidelines for AI, a policy framework developed by policy experts under the auspices of the Public Voice. More than 250 experts and 60 organizations, including the American Association for the Advancement of Science, in 40 countries have endorsed the UGAI. Significant work is also underway at the European Commission, the Council of Europe, several national governments (including Australia, Germany, Japan, South Korea, and the United States) and a joint undertaking between Canada and France that could lead to the establishment of the first international commission on AI.

Many of these frameworks share certain key attributes. Fairness, accuracy, and transparency are reoccurring themes. There is widespread agreement that AI-based decisions should be accountable, though there remains disagreement about how accountability is achieved. Scientists broadly favor replicability, but in the field of machine learning, some have said it may not be possible to reproduce or to even prove outcomes. This perspective has troubling implications for the scientific method and the philosophy of science.

Although we did not include the texts of the General Data Protection Regulation or the Modernized Council of Europe Convention 108+ in this edition, both legal frameworks can be found in EPIC's *Privacy Law Sourcebook* and contain important provisions concerning algorithmic transparency. Articles 13-15 of the GDPR states that individuals are entitled to "meaningful information about the logic involved, as well as the significance and the envisaged" of automated profiling. Article 9(1)(c) of the Council of Europe Privacy Conventions states that every individual has the right "to obtain, on request, knowledge of the reasoning underlying data processing where the results of such processing are applied to him or her." Earlier, the EU Data Protection Directive set out the obligation that every data subject has the right to obtain from the controller "knowledge of the logic involved in any automatic processing of data concerning him at least in the case of the automated decisions [which produces legal effects concerning him or significantly affects him.]" We anticipate the development of significant caselaw and official guidance, based on these provisions, over the next few years.

This compendium focuses on rights-based AI frameworks. In this edition, we have not looked closely at the critical issues of autonomous weapons or AI and job displacement, though some frameworks touch on these policy areas. Both topics are important, and we may explore policy proposals in these domains in more detail in future editions.

Even as we celebrate the significant policy achievements in the AI field over the past year, it is worth stating that there is clear urgency in this work. Business are moving quickly to adopt AI-based systems, often with little understanding of the consequences. Governments are investing massively in AI research and deployment, almost with arms race abandon. While we applaud those governments that have prioritized opportunities for public participation in the development of AI policy, strategic decisions about AI are often made in closed-door meetings with little consideration of those who will be impacted. Opacity now conceals both the algorithm and the policy process.

More broadly, we can begin to see two different scenarios for the AI future. In one, AI augments the work of people, provides new insight into social and

2

economic problems, and offers new solutions that we may choose to adopt based on our own judgement. Fundamental rights, the rule of law, and democratic institutions are secure. In this human-centric view, AI is one of many tools available to society, one of many techniques that enables human progress. But there is also an alternative scenario in which AI displaces the work of people, embeds current social and economic problems, and conceals outcomes in layers of complexity and opacity that humans simply come to accept. The structures that maintain free and open societies begin to diminish. There are clearly important policy choices ahead.

We are grateful for the assistance of many people who have worked with EPIC over the last several years on AI policy. We organized conferences with leading experts and government officials in Brussels and then in Washington. The Brussels conference, *The Public Voice: AI Ethics and Human Rights* featured Professor Anita Allen, TACD's Anna Fielder, Argentina DPA Eduardo Bertoni, Access Now's Fanny Hidvégi, the COE's Dr. Alessandro Mantelero, CNIL President Isabelle Falque-Pierrotin, BEUC's Augustin Reyna, the FTC's Hugh Stevenson, the OECD's Gallia Daor, UK DPA Elizabeth Denham, EDPB Chair Andrea Jelinek, Asociación por los Derechos Civiles's Valeria Milanes, and the Boston Global Forum CEO Nguyen Anh Tuan. The Washington conference, *AI and Human Rights: The Future of AI Policy in the U.S.*, included AAAS CEO Rush Holt, Professor Sherry Turkle, OSTP's Dr. Lynne Parker, the OECD's Sarah Box, Professor Bilyana Petkova, the ACM's Lorraine Kisselburgh, and Professor Harry Lewis. We also want to thank our friends and colleagues with the Aspen Institute AI Roundtable, hosted by Charlie Firestone, and the OECD AI Group of Experts (the "AIGO"), which met over the course of several years and drafted the framework that became the OECD AI Principles, adopted earlier this year. We are grateful to the members of the EPIC Advisory Board who contributed to EPIC's work in support of Algorithmic Transparency, notably Colin Bennett, Christine Borgman, Danielle Citron, Julie Cohen, Simon Davies, David Farber, Michael Froomkin, Woodrow Hartzog, Ian Kerr, Kristina Irion, Joi Ito, Jerry Kang, Lorraine Kisselburgh, Chris Larsen, Alice Marwick, Gary Marx, Mary Minow, Peter G. Neumann, Helen Nissenbaum, Pablo Molina, Cathy O'Neil, Raymond Ozzie, Frank Pasquale, Deborah C. Peel, Stephanie Perrin, Anita Ramasastry, Bruce Schneier, Nadine Strossen, Edward Viltz, James Waldo, Christopher Wolf, Tim Wu, Shoshana Zuboff, and others. We also want to thank our friends at UNESCO for the opportunity to present early work on AI policy. We are particularly grateful to the Patrick J. McGovern Foundation for their support of EPIC's work on AI policy and human rights, and also to Ben Winters is EPIC's Equal Justice Works Fellow Sponsored by the Friends and Family of Philip M. Stern

And a special thanks to EPIC International Counsel Eleni Kyriakides who has compiled much of the material for this volume and who organized EPIC's policy conferences on AI and human rights in Brussels and Washington DC.

Marc Rotenberg
Washington, DC
September 2019

Official AI Guidelines

Organisation for Economic Co-operation and Development, Recommendation of the Council on Artificial Intelligence (2019)

THE COUNCIL,

HAVING REGARD to Article 5 b) of the Convention on the Organisation for Economic Co-operation and Development of 14 December 1960;

HAVING REGARD to the OECD Guidelines for Multinational Enterprises [**OECD/LEGAL/0144**]; Recommendation of the Council concerning Guidelines Governing the Protection of Privacy and Transborder Flows of Personal Data [**OECD/LEGAL/0188**]; Recommendation of the Council concerning Guidelines for Cryptography Policy [**OECD/LEGAL/0289**]; Recommendation of the Council for Enhanced Access and More Effective Use of Public Sector Information [**OECD/LEGAL/0362**]; Recommendation of the Council on Digital Security Risk Management for Economic and Social Prosperity [**OECD/LEGAL/0415**]; Recommendation of the Council on Consumer Protection in E-commerce [**OECD/LEGAL/0422**]; Declaration on the Digital Economy: Innovation, Growth and Social Prosperity (Cancún Declaration) [**OECD/LEGAL/0426**]; Declaration on Strengthening SMEs and Entrepreneurship for Productivity and Inclusive Growth [**OECD/LEGAL/0439**]; as well as the 2016 Ministerial Statement on Building more Resilient and Inclusive Labour Markets, adopted at the OECD Labour and Employment Ministerial Meeting;

HAVING REGARD to the Sustainable Development Goals set out in the 2030 Agenda for Sustainable Development adopted by the United Nations General Assembly (A/RES/70/1) as well as the 1948 Universal Declaration of Human Rights;

HAVING REGARD to the important work being carried out on artificial intelligence (hereafter, "AI") in other international governmental and non-governmental fora;

RECOGNISING that AI has pervasive, far-reaching and global implications that are transforming societies, economic sectors and the world of work, and are likely to increasingly do so in the future;

RECOGNISING that AI has the potential to improve the welfare and well-being of people, to contribute to positive sustainable global economic activity, to increase innovation and productivity, and to help respond to key global challenges;

RECOGNISING that, at the same time, these transformations may have disparate effects within, and between societies and economies, notably regarding economic shifts, competition, transitions in the labour market, inequalities, and implications for democracy and human rights, privacy and data protection, and digital security;

RECOGNISING that trust is a key enabler of digital transformation; that, although the nature of future AI applications and their implications may be hard to foresee, the trustworthiness of AI systems is a key factor for the diffusion and adoption of AI; and that a well-informed whole-of-society public debate is necessary for capturing the beneficial potential of the technology, while limiting the risks associated with it;

UNDERLINING that certain existing national and international legal, regulatory and policy frameworks already have relevance to AI, including those related to human rights, consumer and personal data protection, intellectual property rights, responsible business conduct, and competition, while noting that the appropriateness of some frameworks may need to be assessed and new approaches developed;

RECOGNISING that given the rapid development and implementation of AI, there is a need for a stable policy environment that promotes a human-centric approach to trustworthy AI, that fosters research, preserves economic incentives to innovate, and that applies to all stakeholders according to their role and the context;

CONSIDERING that embracing the opportunities offered, and addressing the challenges raised, by AI applications, and empowering stakeholders to engage is essential to fostering adoption of trustworthy AI in society, and to turning AI trustworthiness into a competitive parameter in the global marketplace;

On the proposal of the Committee on Digital Economy Policy:

    I. **AGREES** that for the purpose of this Recommendation the following terms should be understood as follows:

        —*AI system*: An AI system is a machine-based system that can, for a given set of human-defined objectives, make predictions, recommendations, or decisions influencing real or virtual environments. AI systems are designed to operate with varying levels of autonomy.

–AI system lifecycle: AI system lifecycle phases involve: *i)* 'design, data and models'; which is a context-dependent sequence encompassing planning and design, data collection and processing, as well as model building; *ii)* 'verification and validation'; *iii)* 'deployment'; and *iv)* 'operation and monitoring'. These phases often take place in an iterative manner and are not necessarily sequential. The decision to retire an AI system from operation may occur at any point during the operation and monitoring phase.

–AI knowledge: AI knowledge refers to the skills and resources, such as data, code, algorithms, models, research, know-how, training programmes, governance, processes and best practices, required to understand and participate in the AI system lifecycle.

–AI actors: AI actors are those who play an active role in the AI system lifecycle, including organisations and individuals that deploy or operate AI.

–Stakeholders: Stakeholders encompass all organisations and individuals involved in, or affected by, AI systems, directly or indirectly. AI actors are a subset of stakeholders.

Section 1: Principles for responsible stewardship of trustworthy AI

II. RECOMMENDS that Members and non-Members adhering to this Recommendation (hereafter the "Adherents") promote and implement the following principles for responsible stewardship of trustworthy AI, which are relevant to all stakeholders.

III. CALLS ON all AI actors to promote and implement, according to their respective roles, the following Principles for responsible stewardship of trustworthy AI.

IV. UNDERLINES that the following principles are complementary and should be considered as a whole.

1.1.   Inclusive growth, sustainable development and well-being

Stakeholders should proactively engage in responsible stewardship of trustworthy AI in pursuit of beneficial outcomes for people and the planet, such as augmenting human capabilities and enhancing creativity, advancing inclusion of underrepresented populations, reducing economic, social, gender and other inequalities, and protecting natural environments, thus invigorating inclusive growth, sustainable development and well-being.

1.2. Human-centred values and fairness

a) AI actors should respect the rule of law, human rights and democratic values, throughout the AI system lifecycle. These include freedom, dignity and autonomy, privacy and data protection, non-discrimination and equality, diversity, fairness, social justice, and internationally recognised labour rights.

b) To this end, AI actors should implement mechanisms and safeguards, such as capacity for human determination, that are appropriate to the context and consistent with the state of art.

1.3. Transparency and explainability

AI Actors should commit to transparency and responsible disclosure regarding AI systems. To this end, they should provide meaningful information, appropriate to the context, and consistent with the state of art:

i.to foster a general understanding of AI systems,

ii.to make stakeholders aware of their interactions with AI systems, including in the workplace,

iii.to enable those affected by an AI system to understand the outcome, and,

iv.to enable those adversely affected by an AI system to challenge its outcome based on plain and easy-to-understand information on the factors, and the logic that served as the basis for the prediction, recommendation or decision.

1.4. Robustness, security and safety

a) AI systems should be robust, secure and safe throughout their entire lifecycle so that, in conditions of normal use, foreseeable use or misuse, or other adverse conditions, they function appropriately and do not pose unreasonable safety risk.

b) To this end, AI actors should ensure traceability, including in relation to datasets, processes and decisions made during the AI system lifecycle, to enable analysis of the AI system's outcomes and responses to inquiry, appropriate to the context and consistent with the state of art.

c) AI actors should, based on their roles, the context, and their ability to act, apply a systematic risk management approach to each phase of the AI system lifecycle on a continuous basis to address risks related to AI systems, including privacy, digital security, safety and bias.

1.5. Accountability

AI actors should be accountable for the proper functioning of AI systems and for the respect of the above principles, based on their roles, the context, and consistent with the state of art.

Section 2: National policies and international co-operation for trustworthy AI

V. RECOMMENDS that Adherents implement the following recommendations, consistent with the principles in section 1, in their national policies and international co-operation, with special attention to small and medium-sized enterprises (SMEs).

2.1. Investing in AI research and development

a) Governments should consider long-term public investment, and encourage private investment, in research and development, including interdisciplinary efforts, to spur innovation in trustworthy AI that focus on challenging technical issues and on AI-related social, legal and ethical implications and policy issues.

b) Governments should also consider public investment and encourage private investment in open datasets that are representative and respect privacy and data protection to support an environment for AI research and development that is free of inappropriate bias and to improve interoperability and use of standards.

2.2. Fostering a digital ecosystem for AI

Governments should foster the development of, and access to, a digital ecosystem for trustworthy AI. Such an ecosystem includes in particular digital technologies and infrastructure, and mechanisms for sharing AI knowledge, as appropriate. In this regard, governments should consider promoting mechanisms, such as data trusts, to support the safe, fair, legal and ethical sharing of data.

2.3. Shaping an enabling policy environment for AI

a) Governments should promote a policy environment that supports an agile transition from the research and development stage to the deployment and operation stage for trustworthy AI systems. To this effect, they should consider using experimentation to provide a controlled environment in which AI systems can be tested, and scaled-up, as appropriate.

b) Governments should review and adapt, as appropriate, their policy and regulatory frameworks and assessment mechanisms as they apply to AI systems to encourage innovation and competition for trustworthy AI.

2.4. Building human capacity and preparing for labour market transformation

a) Governments should work closely with stakeholders to prepare for the transformation of the world of work and of society. They should empower people to effectively use and interact with AI systems across the breadth of applications, including by equipping them with the necessary skills.

b) Governments should take steps, including through social dialogue, to ensure a fair transition for workers as AI is deployed, such as through training programmes along the working life, support for those affected by displacement, and access to new opportunities in the labour market.

c) Governments should also work closely with stakeholders to promote the responsible use of AI at work, to enhance the safety of workers and the quality of jobs, to foster entrepreneurship and productivity, and aim to ensure that the benefits from AI are broadly and fairly shared.

2.5. International co-operation for trustworthy AI

a) Governments, including developing countries and with stakeholders, should actively co-operate to advance these principles and to progress on responsible stewardship of trustworthy AI.

b) Governments should work together in the OECD and other global and regional fora to foster the sharing of AI knowledge, as appropriate. They should encourage international, cross-sectoral and open multi-stakeholder initiatives to garner long-term expertise on AI.

c) Governments should promote the development of multi-stakeholder, consensus-driven global technical standards for interoperable and trustworthy AI.

d) Governments should also encourage the development, and their own use, of internationally comparable metrics to measure AI research, development and deployment, and gather the evidence base to assess progress in the implementation of these principles.

VI. INVITES the Secretary-General and Adherents to disseminate this Recommendation.

VII. INVITES non-Adherents to take due account of, and adhere to, this Recommendation.

VIII. INSTRUCTS the Committee on Digital Economy Policy:

a) to continue its important work on artificial intelligence building on this Recommendation and taking into account work in other international fora, and to further develop the measurement framework for evidence-based AI policies;

b) to develop and iterate further practical guidance on the implementation of this Recommendation, and to report to the Council on progress made no later than end December 2019;

c) to provide a forum for exchanging information on AI policy and activities including experience with the implementation of this Recommendation, and to foster multi-stakeholder and interdisciplinary dialogue to promote trust in and adoption of AI; and d)to monitor, in consultation with other relevant Committees, the implementation of this Recommendation and report thereon to the Council no later than five years following its adoption and regularly thereafter.

Background Information

The Recommendation on Artificial Intelligence (AI) – the first intergovernmental standard on AI – was adopted by the OECD Council at Ministerial level on 22 May 2019 on the proposal of the Committee on Digital Economy Policy (CDEP). The Recommendation aims to foster innovation and trust in AI by promoting the responsible stewardship of trustworthy AI while ensuring respect for human rights and democratic values. Complementing existing OECD standards in areas such as privacy, digital security risk management, and responsible business conduct, the Recommendation focuses on AI-specific issues and sets a standard that is implementable and sufficiently flexible to stand the test of time in this rapidly evolving field. In June 2019, at the Osaka Summit, G20 Leaders welcomed G20 AI Principles, drawn from the OECD Recommendation.

The Recommendation identifies five complementary values-based principles for the responsible stewardship of trustworthy AI and calls on AI actors to promote and implement them:

- inclusive growth, sustainable development and well-being;

- human-centred values and fairness;

- transparency and explainability;

- robustness, security and safety;

- and accountability.

In addition to and consistent with these value-based principles, the Recommendation also provides five recommendations to policy-makers pertaining to national policies and international co-operation for trustworthy AI, namely:

- investing in AI research and development;

- fostering a digital ecosystem for AI;

- shaping an enabling policy environment for AI;

- building human capacity and preparing for labour market transformation;

- and international co-operation for trustworthy AI.

The Recommendation also includes a provision for the development of metrics to measure AI research, development and deployment, and for building an evidence base to assess progress in its implementation.

The OECD's work on Artificial Intelligence and rationale for developing the OECD Recommendation on Artificial Intelligence

Artificial Intelligence (AI) is a general-purpose technology that has the potential to improve the welfare and well-being of people, to contribute to positive sustainable global economic activity, to increase innovation and productivity, and to help respond to key global challenges. It is deployed in many sectors ranging from production, finance and transport to healthcare and security.

Alongside benefits, AI also raises challenges for our societies and economies, notably regarding economic shifts and inequalities, competition, transitions in the labour market, and implications for democracy and human rights.

The OECD has undertaken empirical and policy activities on AI in support of the policy debate over the past two years, starting with a Technology Foresight Forum on AI in 2016 and an international conference on *AI: Intelligent Machines, Smart Policies* in 2017. The Organisation also conducted analytical and measurement work that provides an overview of the AI technical landscape, maps economic and social impacts of AI technologies and their applications, identifies major policy considerations, and describes AI initiatives from governments and other stakeholders at national and international levels.

This work has demonstrated the need to shape a stable policy environment at the international level to foster trust in and adoption of AI in society. Against this background, the OECD Committee on Digital Economy Policy (CDEP) agreed to develop a draft Council Recommendation to promote a human-centric approach to trustworthy AI, that fosters research, preserves economic incentives to innovate, and applies to all stakeholders.

Complementing existing OECD standards already relevant to AI – such as those on privacy and data protection, digital security risk management, and responsible business conduct – the Recommendation focuses on policy issues that are specific to AI and strives to set a standard that is implementable and flexible enough to stand the test of time in a rapidly evolving field. The Recommendation contains five high-level values-based principles and five recommendations for national policies and international co-operation. It also proposes a common understanding of key terms, such as "AI system" and "AI actors", for the purposes of the Recommendation.

More specifically, the Recommendation includes two substantive sections:

1. **Principles for responsible stewardship of trustworthy AI**: the first section sets out five complementary principles relevant to all stakeholders: *i)* inclusive growth, sustainable development and well-being; *ii)* human-centred values and fairness; *iii)* transparency and explainability; *iv)* robustness, security and safety; and *v)* accountability. This section further calls on AI actors to promote and implement these principles according to their roles.

2. **National policies and international co-operation for trustworthy AI**: consistent with the five aforementioned principles, this section provides five recommendations to Members and non-Members having adhered to the draft Recommendation (hereafter the "Adherents") to implement in their national policies and international co-operation: *i)* investing in AI research and development; *ii)* fostering a digital ecosystem for AI; *iii)* shaping an enabling policy environment for AI; *iv)* building human capacity and preparing for labour market transformation; and *v)* international co-operation for trustworthy AI.

An inclusive and participatory process for developing the Recommendation

The development of the Recommendation was participatory in nature, incorporating input from a broad range of sources throughout the process. In May 2018, the CDEP agreed to form an expert group to scope principles to foster trust in and adoption of AI, with a view to developing a draft Council Recommendation in the course of 2019. The AI Group of experts at the OECD (AIGO) was subsequently established, comprising over 50 experts from different disciplines and different sectors (government, industry, civil society, trade unions, the technical community and academia) - see **http://www.oecd.org/going-digital/ai/oecd-aigo-membership-list.pdf** for the full list. Between September 2018 and February 2019 the group held four meetings: in Paris, France, in September and November 2018, in Cambridge, MA, United States, at the Massachusetts Institute of Technology (MIT) in January 2019, back to back with the MIT AI Policy Congress, and finally in Dubai, United Arab Emirates, at the World Government Summit in February 2019. The work benefited from the diligence, engagement and substantive contributions of the experts participating in AIGO, as well as from their multi-stakeholder and multidisciplinary backgrounds.

Drawing on the final output document of the AIGO, a draft Recommendation was developed in the CDEP and with the consultation of other relevant OECD bodies. The CDEP approved a final draft Recommendation and agreed to transmit it to the OECD Council for adoption in a special meeting on 14-15 March 2019. The OECD Council adopted the Recommendation at its meeting at Ministerial level on 22-23 May 2019.

Follow-up, monitoring of implementation and dissemination tools

The OECD Recommendation on AI provides the first intergovernmental standard for AI policies and a foundation on which to conduct further analysis and develop tools to support governments in their implementation efforts. In this regard, it instructs the CDEP to monitor the implementation of the Recommendation and report to the Council on its implementation and continued relevance five years after its adoption and regularly thereafter. The CDEP is also instructed to continue its work on AI, building on this Recommendation, and taking into account work in other international fora, such as UNESCO, the European Union, the Council of Europe and the initiative to build an International Panel on AI (see https://pm.gc.ca/eng/news/2018/12/06/mandate-international-panel-artificial-intelligence and https://www.gouvernement.fr/en/france-and-canada-create-new-expert-international-panel-on-artificial-intelligence).

In order to support implementation of the Recommendation, the Council instructed the CDEP to develop practical guidance for implementation, to provide a forum for exchanging information on AI policy and activities, and to foster multi-stakeholder and interdisciplinary dialogue. This will be achieved largely through the OECD AI Policy Observatory, an inclusive hub for public policy on AI that aims to help countries encourage, nurture and monitor the responsible development of trustworthy artificial intelligence systems for the benefit of society. It will combine resources from across the OECD with those of partners from all stakeholder groups to provide multidisciplinary, evidence-based policy analysis on AI. The Observatory is planned to be launched late 2019 and will include a live database of AI strategies, policies and initiatives that countries and other stakeholders can share and update, enabling the comparison of their key elements in an interactive manner. It will also be continuously updated with AI metrics, measurements, policies and good practices that could lead to further updates in the practical guidance for implementation.

The Recommendation is open to non-OECD Member adherence, underscoring the global relevance of OECD AI policy work as well as the Recommendation's call for international co-operation.

International Working Group on Data Protection in Telecommunications,
Working Paper on Privacy and Artificial Intelligence (2018)[1]

Introduction

1. Artificial intelligence (AI) is high on the agenda of most sectors due to its perceived potential for radically improving services, commercial breakthroughs and financial gains. Over the next five years, it is expected that there will be mass implementation of AI across multiple sectors. However, enthusiasm for the opportunities offered by AI must be tempered by careful consideration of AI's impact on individual rights to privacy and data protection.

2. Recent advances in AI can be explained by the convergence of several factors including the development of innovative machine learning methods, the increase in available computational power and the availability of more labelled data, allowing the creation of complex statistical models.

3. AI systems in general, and machine learning technologies in particular, generally require the processing of huge volumes of data for their development. In a number of cases, this data is personal data, potentially impacting individuals' rights to data protection and to privacy.

Scope

4. The purpose of this working paper is to highlight the privacy challenges associated with the development and use of AI, and to provide a set of technical recommendations to help different stakeholders mitigate privacy risks when implementing it. While the use of AI also raises other ethical and societal concerns which deserve analysis, these are outside the scope of the present working paper.[2]

5. This paper focuses on some of the different ways in which AI interacts with personal data such as:

---

[1] The Office of the Privacy Commissioner of Canada abstains from the adoption of this Working Paper.

[2] Internationally, Governments, Data Protection Agencies, and laws have variously sought to incorporate ethical frameworks, human rights controls and other guidance related to AI. While we encourage consultation with and implementation of appropriate guidance, questions of fairness and ethics are touched on but fall outside the scope of this paper.

- the use of personal data in algorithmic training/learning;

- the application of AI to personal data (e.g., for decision-making purposes); and

- the use of AI to extract personal data from data sets which superficially appear not to contain personal data.

6. This paper is intended for developers of AI systems, system providers, organisations purchasing and using AI systems, and for data protection authorities.[3]

Definitions[4]

7. Artificial Intelligence

AI is a term that has no universally accepted definition. AI can be described as the theory and development of computer systems able to perform tasks normally requiring human intelligence, such as visual perception, speech recognition, decision-making, and translation between languages.

8. Specific vs. general AI

AI systems are currently developed for specific purposes. Some examples of the specific purposes for which AI is being used are: profiling, classification, image recognition, natural language processing and autonomous machines. So-called "general AI", where one system is able to solve different types of problems, much like the human brain, is currently an unsolved challenge and this working paper will not address it.

9. Machine learning (ML)

ML is a subset of AI that uses statistical techniques to give computer systems the ability to "learn" from data with the goal of deriving an algorithm for the solution of

---

[3] *Developers of AI systems* refers to private and public organisations and research institutions pursuing AI research and development. System providers are organisations and research institutions that use basic technologies developed by others (i.e., organisations that use AI in their own projects or in solutions supplied by others). These can be data controllers or merely a supplier of a service or product. Organisations purchasing and using AI systems may be both private and public organisations.

[4] This section is not intended to provide comprehensive or authoritative definitions of AI concepts, but seeks to delineate the understanding of these concepts that underlies the analysis and recommendations of this paper.

a task without being given explicit instruction. The terms artificial intelligence and machine learning are often used as synonyms even though they are conceptually different.

10. Neural Network

Neural networks are largely inspired by our understanding of the way the human brain functions. These networks are built using what is basically a very simple component, an artificial neuron, which has a variable number of inputs and one output. Each input to an artificial neuron has a weight value that determines the extent of its influence on the final result. These values are adjusted when the network is trained to give the desired results.

11. Deep learning

Deep Learning is part of a broad family of machine learning methods based on data representations. As of today, it is almost exclusively based on neural networks. The deep part in deep learning is based on the number of layers found in the neural network. When a neural network has more than one (hidden) layer between the input and output layers, it is commonly viewed as deep.

How algorithms learn

12. There are three main forms of machine learning:

- Supervised learning

Supervised [*sic*] learning involves the use of labelled data. If the data includes images, the label may include information about the contents of each image, for example indicating if a dog or a cat is pictured.

The data set is typically split in two, the larger part being used to train the model, the remaining part being used to test how precisely the model categorizes new data. The model requires a certain degree of generalisation to avoid overfitting. An overfitted model is too well adjusted, meaning it will perform very well with training data but poorly with new data.

Learning/training takes place as follows:

a. A set of labelled data is required.

b. Depending on data type, and what is considered relevant, the features (attributes of input data) to be used for learning are selected. The data is labelled to denote the correct prediction/answer.

c. A model is built that, based on the same features, will attempt to predict/produce the right label for unknown data.

d. The utility of the model is assessed using the part of the data set aside for that purpose. If results are unsatisfactory, the training process is renewed.

When in use after training, new and unlabelled data is fed into the system and a result is produced that should correspond with what the model learned during the training phase.

- Unsupervised learning

In unsupervised learning, the aim is to develop models that can detect patterns that would enable subsequent sets of unlabeled data to be clustered. If the training data consists of images of cats and dogs without any descriptive labels, the goal would be for these data to be sorted into two clusters sharing similar features – one consisting of images of dogs, and the other of cat images. However, the AI system will not be able to identify the nature of the two clusters, meaning that the system does not know that it sees images of cats and dogs.

Learning proceeds as follows:

a. A dataset is used in which there must be a certain number of similarities, or patterns, if it is to be meaningful.

b. The machine-learning algorithm will produce clusters based on similarities/patterns in the dataset.

c. A model is built that will sort, segregate, segment, cluster, etc. data using the patterns found during training.

When in use, the model will identify which group the new images belong to.

A disadvantage with this method is that the model cannot place data in groups other than those discovered during the learning process. It is therefore very important that the training data represents all possible clusters that new data might possibly belong to. Otherwise there is a risk that data could be forced into clusters where they do not belong, or that the data may simply not be clustered at all.

- Reinforcement learning

Reinforcement learning is based on trial and error. It allows machines and software agents to determine the optimal behaviour within a specific context in order to maximize performance - the model learns which actions are targeted towards the goal. While this reinforcement may use a pre-compiled set of data points as a starting point, the training phase may also proceed by immediately interacting with the real world domain, or acting upon computer generated responses. This means that less data, or no data at all, may be needed for the system to learn.

13. At some point during the learning process, there will be a need to assess the utility of the model to determine if it is meeting the specified requirements or goals (e.g., is the model consistently producing a correct/proper label for unknown data?). This can be done by measuring the quality of the segmentation, clustering etc. achieved by the model, by applying the model to new objects, and manually verifying the classification performed.

14. <u>Different levels of complexity and intelligibility</u> There are several types of machine learning systems available or under development, each having different levels of complexity and intelligibility, which are adapted to solve various problems, and which require different amounts of data in order to learn.

15. A decision tree is one of the simplest and most popular forms of machine learning algorithms. Simply put, a decision tree is a tree in which each branch node represents a choice between a number of alternatives and each leaf node represents a decision. Decision trees train themselves, learning from given examples and predicting for unseen circumstances. The decision tree model might not be the best choice to analyse vast amounts of data, but it does offer a high degree of intelligibility. It is possible to follow the outline of the tree and see the criteria on which the result is based. With increasing amounts of data, however, a point will be reached where it will be difficult to obtain an overview and understanding of the decision-making process.

16. On the other end of the complexity scale, there are deep artificial neural networks. A neural network consists of a large number of artificial neurons arranged in more than two layers.[5] The models are based on weights and biases that are learned during training in something called backpropagation. Unlike normal programming statements or decision trees, the nature of the numeric values and the size of the networks can make it hard to understand how a decision is reached.

---

[5] In 2016 Microsoft won an image recognition competition using a network consisting of 152 layers (https://blogs.microsoft.com/ai/2015/12/10/microsoft-researchers-win-imagenet-computer-vision-challenge)

When data is passed through the network, it is difficult to see how the information is combined and weighted to produce the final result.

17. Because some data must be viewed in context to make sense, for example words in the case of machine translation of speech transcription, some neural networks have a form of short-term memory. This allows them to produce different outputs based on the data that was processed previously, which of course makes it more difficult to determine how a result was derived. This also means that it can be very difficult to merely examine the algorithms to find out how they work and what decisions they reach.

Examples of AI in practice

18. <u>Image recognition and analysis</u>

Image recognition and analysis is an application of AI that has already been put to commercial use. These kinds of systems can recognize objects or people (e.g., image labelling or facial recognition), infer emotional states of people (e.g., facial gesture recognition) or detect and track a certain object or person through a video sequence.

> **Example:** An application which runs on Pivothead glasses aims to help visually-impaired individuals understand the world around them. When the wearer touches a sensor on the glasses, an image of their surroundings is captured, analyzed, and verbally described. For instance, if the system detects a person in the image, it can describe their approximate age, gender, facial emotion, and/or current activity. Similarly, if an image of text (a menu, news article, etc.) is captured, it is read back to the user.[6]

19. In facial recognition, a picture of a face is used to measure specific characteristics (i.e., nodal points on the face, such as the distance between the eyes or the shape of the cheekbones) and a template is produced. The trained algorithm compares this template to existing templates for categorisation, identification or authentication purposes. It should be noted that these systems are not infallible – they may incorrectly categorize, identify or authenticate an individual (i.e., a false positive error) or they may fail to categorize, identify or authenticate an individual (i.e., a false negative error).

---

[6] The Pivothead application is capable of more than describing an individual within the image or reading text. According to the case study linked via the Pivothead website the application can also describe scenery. http://www.pivothead.com/seeingai/

> **Example:** The Chinese police have successfully tested smart glasses in conjunction with a facial recognition system to match travellers on a railway station with criminal suspects. According to the company that developed the technology, the system can identify faces from a database of 10,000 persons in 100 milliseconds.[7]

> **Example:** In 2015, it was revealed that the Google Photos service mistakenly tagged black people as "gorillas". After the incident, the company promised "immediate action" to prevent any repetition of the error. That action has been to censor "gorilla", as well as chimpanzee and monkey, from searches and image tags. That's the conclusion drawn by Wired magazine, which tested more than 40,000 images of animals on the service. Photos accurately tagged images of pandas and poodles, but consistently returned no results for the great apes and monkeys – despite accurately finding baboons, gibbons and orangutans.[8]

> **Example:** In the UK, the police are experimenting with facial recognition technology. According to a report from Big Brother Watch, the police's use of this technology to recognize people is failing, with the wrong person being identified nine times out ten. South Wales police have been given two million pounds to test the technology, but so far it gets it wrong 91% of the time. The UK's Metropolitan Police used facial recognition at the 2017 Notting Hill carnival and the system was wrong 98% of the time, falsely telling officers on 102 occasions it had spotted a suspect.[9]

20. Natural language processing (NLP) NLP systems use AI to allow people to interact with computers by speech or chat. This involves natural language and speech recognition and generation.

---

[7] The Independent, "Chinese police are using facial-recognition glasses to scan travelers", 2018

http://www.independent.co.uk/news/world/asia/china-police-facial-recognition-sunglasses-security-smart-tech-travellers-criminals-a8206491.html

[8] Wired, "When it comes to gorillas, Google Photos remains blind", 2018,
https://www.wired.com/story/when-it-comes-to-gorillas-google-photos-remains-blind/

[9] The Guardian, "UK police use of facial recognition technology a failure, says report", 2018,
https://www.theguardian.com/uk-news/2018/may/15/uk-police-use-of-facial-recognition-technology-failure

> **Example:** There are many products on the market using natural language processing. Some of the most popular are voice assistants like Google's Assistant, Apple's Siri, Amazon Alexa or Microsoft's Cortana, automated translation services like Google Translate, DeepL or Bing Translator or chatbots such as 1-800-Flowers and Swelly.

Note that models for speech recognition that are trained to recognize speech by individual speakers may contain personal data both on the semantic level (particular phrases used by a particular speaker), and on the phonetic level (manner of articulation of a particular speaker).

21. The development of AI systems capable of processing natural language makes it possible to collect and process data stored in audio or video recordings, or in images of text on paper. AI systems that interact with humans using natural language may use those interactions for learning and further development of the natural language capabilities of AI systems.

22. Autonomous machines

Autonomous machines are intelligent machines capable of performing tasks in the world by themselves, without explicit human control. Different features of AI may be applied in autonomous machines - natural language processing allows for direct interaction between humans and machines, while image recognition and audio analysis allow autonomous machines to recognize their environment. The accuracy requirements in decisions made by autonomous machines are often high.

> **Example:** Self-driving cars like the ones under development by Waymo, Uber or Tesla, home cleaning robots like Roomba or unmanned surveillance drones, are examples of autonomous machines.

23. Automated individual decision-making and profiling AI systems and machine learning are increasingly used to automate individual decision-making and profiling. Profiling and automated decision-making can be very useful for organisations in many sectors, including healthcare, education, financial services and marketing. They can lead to quicker and more consistent decisions, particularly in cases where a very large volume of data needs to be analysed and decisions made very quickly. Although these techniques can be useful, there are potential risks.

24. **Profiling** is any form of automated processing that uses personal data to evaluate certain aspects of an individual, such as personality, behavior, interests and habits to make predictions or decisions about them. Profiling may use AI and machine learning to create algorithms that find correlations between separate datasets, or between various personal attributes, and the observed behavior of

individuals. These algorithms can be used to make a wide range of decisions, for example predicting behavior or controlling access to a service.

Example: Several loan companies are using algorithms that factor in social media activity to determine whether to make a credit offer. A German company called Kreditech deploys a proprietary credit-scoring algorithm to process up to 20,000 data points on the loan applicant's social media networks, e-commerce behavior, and web analytics. Information about the applicant's social media friends is collected to assess the applicant's "decision-making quality" and creditworthiness.[10] In India and Russia, Fair Isaac Corp ("FICO") is partnering with startups like Lenddo to process large quantities of data from the applicant's mobile phone to conduct predictive credit-risk assessments. Lenddo collects longitudinal location data to verify the applicant's residence and work address, as well as analyzing the applicant's interpersonal communications and associations on social media to produce a credit score.[11]

---

25. **Automated decision-making** is the process of making a decision by automated means without any human involvement. These decisions can be based on factual data, as well as on digitally created profiles or inferred data. Examples of this include an online decision to award a loan or an aptitude test used for recruitment which uses pre-programmed algorithms and criteria. Automated decision-making often involves profiling. Not all profiling is used for decision-making purposes; nevertheless, the overlap between these two practices is considerable.

Example: To predict the likelihood that a convicted person will reoffend, some correctional institutions in the United States use AI systems for profiling based on data on the convict's education, family background and social functioning, among other information.[12] Algorithms are also deployed in the criminal justice system to set bail, assess forensic evidence, and determine sentences and parole opportunities.[13] Several states use proprietary commercial algorithms, which may not be subject to open government laws, to make such determinations.

---

[10] https://www.kreditech.com/

[11] https://www.lenddo.com/

[12] See, for example COMPAS, https://www.cdcr.ca.gov/rehabilitation/docs/FS_COMPAS_Final_4-15-09.pdf or https://doc.wi.gov/Pages/AboutDOC/COMPAS.aspx

[13] See, for example, The New York Times, "Sent to prison by a Software program's Secret Algorithms", 2017, https://www.nytimes.com/2017/05/01/us/politics/sent-to-prison-by-a-software-programs-secret-algorithms.html, and EPIC.org, "EPIC – Algorithms in the Criminal Justice System", https://epic.org/algorithmic-transparency/crim-justice, for more general information.

Privacy challenges

26. The intensive use of data involved in many forms of AI, and the new data processing opportunities it brings, challenge fundamental data protection principles.[14] This paper highlights the most relevant challenges regarding privacy and the processing of personal data. While the use of AI also raises other ethical and societal concerns which deserve analysis, these are not within the scope of the present working paper.

27. <u>Unlawful bias and discrimination</u>

One of the major privacy challenges of AI systems is bias. Some data sets used to train machine learning-based and artificial intelligence systems have been found to contain inherent bias resulting in decisions that can unfairly discriminate against certain individuals or groups.

28. The fairness principle requires all processing of personal data to respect the data subject's legitimate interests, and that the data be used in accordance with what he or she might reasonably expect. The processing of personal data by an AI system may not respect the data subject's interests, or align with the data subject's reasonable expectations, especially if the algorithm is biased in some way, resulting in decisions or predictions with a discriminatory impact.

> **Example:** A research study found substantial disparities in the accuracy of three commercial face recognition systems conducting automated facial analysis. The study found that the commercial systems' training data were overwhelmingly composed of lighter-skinned subjects. The study showed that facial recognition of darker-skinned females had error rates of over 30 %, compared to an error rate of 0.8% for lighter-skinned males.[15]

29. However, having a non-biased training dataset is not enough. For example, even if an AI system is not given input on sensitive attributes in an attempt to avoid discriminatory treatment, it is still possible for it to develop a compromised model on the basis of the information available that may in turn result in an unwanted discriminatory outcome. It is necessary to conduct an assessment of the results to make sure that there are no discriminatory effects.

---

[14] See, for example GDPR Article 5.

[15] Buolamwin, Joy and Timnit Gebru, "Gender Shades: Intersectional Accuracy Disparities in Commercial Gender Classification", Proceedings of Machine Learning Research 81:1–15, 2018, http://proceedings.mlr.press/v81/buolamwini18a/buolamwini18a.pdf

30. There may be many reasons why individuals are underrepresented in data sets. For example, individuals may be very careful about what information they reveal about themselves, resulting in a lack of data to include in the data set. Similarly, they may not have access to or fluency in the technology that generates data about their activities and behaviors. Individuals may be deemed to be of less interest from a data perspective for some reason (e.g., they may not be in a certain economic class), resulting in their data not being included in the data set. Whatever the reason for their lack of inclusion, the result is that the AI system may exhibit bias against them.

31. AI systems use mathematically defined fairness and equity metrics to measure possible bias. The metrics used in the design of an AI system will deeply influence the outcomes of the AI system. However, it is not possible to design an AI system that is fair according to all metrics. Consequently, the metrics used should be part of the information provided to the users of AI systems in order to meet transparency obligations.

32. Even with concerted effort, it may be impossible to avoid bias in the output of an AI system. In some instances, there may not be any data available that is without inherent bias. Even when the most thorough efforts are made to avoid any bias in the selection of data, the data would reflect any bias which is present in social reality. In some fields, the state of knowledge may be insufficient to recognize bias in datasets or algorithms. Bias could also be ingrained in generally accepted principles of reasoning which have never been subject to thorough scrutiny. The lack of unbiased datasets in a domain should prevent the development of AI systems in that domain, as those systems will produce biased results.

33. Data Maximisation vs. the Principle of Data Minimisation

The ability to sift through and analyse vast amounts of data holds great potential for advancement in areas such as disease related research or personalised services across sectors. In the search for new connections and more precise analyses, it is tempting to give the system access to as much data as possible – this is sometimes called "data maximisation". If the data used is personal data, this contradicts the principle of data minimisation.

34. The data minimisation principle requires that data be adequate, relevant, proportionate to the purpose for which it is collected, and limited to what is necessary for achieving that purpose. The capabilities that AI systems provide are pushing the limits for what is relevant, and the push to provide more and more data to facilitate connections pushes the data minimisation principle. Data may become newly meaningful in company with other data, greater processing capacity and deeper analyses. However, the potential for profit, research breakthroughs and more

efficient services needs to be balanced with the potential risks and infringements that the extensive use of personal data has for individuals' privacy and human rights.

35. Erosion of purpose limitation

The purpose limitation principle means that the reason for processing personal data must be clearly established and indicated at the time the data is collected. Furthermore, personal data cannot be re-used for incompatible purposes – uses must meet individuals' reasonable expectations unless the re-use is explicitly mandated by law. This is essential if the individual is to have and exercise control over his/her information.

36. A challenge when developing AI is that it often requires many different types of personal data – information that in some cases has been collected for other purposes. Consider, for example, speech recordings made (on the basis of consent) for the improvement of the operation of voice-operated devices. These recordings could be used to train algorithms which seek to predict information about the health of the speaker. Such re-purposing of information may be useful and provide more accurate analyses than those which were technically feasible previously, but it can also be in contravention of the purpose limitation principle.

37. In addition, more powerful analytical tools might make it more tempting to use data for new purposes in order to enhance the output value. Economic and social benefits might be drivers to reuse data for new purposes.

38. Lack of transparency and intelligibility

Data protection is largely about safeguarding the right of individuals to decide how information about themselves is used. This requires that data controllers are open about the use of personal data, and provide necessary information about the processing.

39. Transparent artificial intelligence systems are ones in which it is possible to know how and why a system made a particular decision. The term transparency also addresses the concepts of intelligibility, and interpretability. Transparency enhances accountability.

40. It can be challenging to satisfy the transparency principle in AI powered decision-making systems. One reason is that the details behind an algorithm's functioning are often considered proprietary information, and so are closely guarded by their owners. Another reason is that, depending on the AI system, the

algorithms might be so complex that even their creators do not know exactly how they work in practice.[16] This is AI's so-called black box problem.

41. If AI systems operate like black boxes and cannot be tested independently, the algorithms may be outside the scope of meaningful scrutiny and accountability. If organizations who use these systems for making automated decisions (as discussed earlier in the paper) are unwilling or unable to explain those decisions, then the individuals will have no way of knowing upon what information the decision was made, or whether the decisions were accurate, fair, or even about them. It will also be difficult for any individual to challenge or contest the decision. To protect individual rights in these situations, persons must be provided both the logic of the processing and an explanation of the automated decision-making.[17] Further, a lack of transparency and intelligibility in AI systems will also make it difficult for supervisory authorities (of any kind) to investigate, audit and inspect the systems.

42. Depending on the specific purpose of the AI, the inability to explain how a decision was reached could legally prevent the use of the system. For example, if social services denies an individual access to a social welfare benefit, many jurisdictions have a legal requirement to explain how that decision was made. The obligation to provide an explanation of how a decision is reached is also evident in some jurisdictions' privacy legislation.[18]

43. Finally, the black box problem makes it difficult to detect and remedy bias or security breaches in the processes. For example, detecting a data poisoning attack (poisoning the training data by injecting false data to compromise the learning process) may be impossible in a scenario where there is no explanation for the outcome of an AI system.

44. Erosion of consent

A lack of transparency in AI-powered systems, combined with a lack of intelligibility, may significantly erode the meaningfulness of consent. For consent

---

[16] Creators know how their systems work theoretically (they implement methods such as gradient descent that should optimize the way the system work) but in practice the huge number of parameters and their automated tuning based on the statistical properties of the data make it hard to be able to precisely explain why such a decision was made, why such a parameter is so high while another is so low, etc.

[17] See GDPR Article 5 on Principles relating to processing (listing transparency as fundamental requirement for all processing of personal data); Article 13(2)(f) and 14(2)(g) on the Right to be informed; Article 15 on Right of access

[18] See for example GDPR Article 22 on Automated decision-making

to be valid, it shall be freely given, specific and informed. If individuals do not know how their data is going to be processed, and no-one can explain it to them, they will not be in a position to give a meaningful consent to the collection and processing of their data. In cases where a system does not depend on the availability of a specific individual's data, individuals could nevertheless face a loss of control over their data even if they refrain from providing consent. Examples of such situations include where individuals who have given their consent possess similar attributes as individuals who have not consented to the data processing, and yet this data is used to infer information or make decisions about those who have not consented.

45. Data analyses might uncover sensitive information

AI's vast analytical power is able to combine and analyse different information elements, which may not be sensitive in themselves, but when combined may generate a sensitive result. For instance, AI might identify patterns that can predict individual's dispositions, for example related to health, political viewpoints or sexual orientation. This kind of information is subject to special protection.

46. Similarly, inappropriate use of AI may weaken the effectiveness of consumer choice. By using data from consumers who opt in or decline to opt out of interacting with an AI system, that system can be employed to infer information about similarly-situated individuals who choose not to interact with those systems and do not share their data.

47. Risk of re-identification

Due to the ability of AI systems to process a wide variety of data from a multiplicity of sources, the use of AI may magnify the risk that individuals become identifiable in data sets, including data sets used for training purposes[19], which previously appeared to be anonymous. This is particularly true where data from different sources are combined and processed on a large scale. This makes anonymisation less likely to be successfully achieved. Thus it becomes ever more difficult to determine whether a data set is sufficiently and robustly anonymized, a process to which AI contributes for two reasons:

> - The term "to identify" - and thus "to anonymize" - is complicated. Individuals may be identified in many different ways.[20] This includes direct

---

[19] Veale M, Binns R, Edwards L., "Algorithms that remember: model inversion attacks and data protection law", Phil. Trans. R. Society, 2018, http://dx.doi.org/10.1098/rsta.2018.0083

[20] The Article 29 Data Protection Working Party, Opinion 05/2014 on "Anonymisation Techniques".

identification, in which case a person will be explicitly identifiable by a single attribute (for example, their full name), and indirect identification, in which two or more data attributes describing physical, physiological, genetic, mental, economic, cultural or social characteristics must be combined in order to allow for the identification or singling out of individuals in a larger group. AI algorithms have the potential to uncover these characteristics from more idiosyncratic information (e.g. by uncovering a person's sexual identity from seemingly innocuous data); and

- Companies that use what is assumed to be an anonymized data set will not know for certain whether or not there are other external data sets available whose acquisition will make it possible to re-identify individuals in the data set. These acquisitions are becoming more routine in the quest for ever more powerful AI algorithms.

48. Information security risk

AI faces the risk of adversarial "injection" where third parties transmit malicious data to a learning AI system that in turns disrupts a neural network's functionality. For instance, a group of researchers confused an image recognition system by slightly modifying images used to train a system built to recognize road signs; the trained networks in question then misclassified almost all of the road signs a correctly trained algorithm recognized.[21]

49. The processing of personal data by an AI system in itself yields security risks. Like any other IT system, AI is vulnerable to security breaches. Searching out and exploiting those systems might be particularly attractive if malicious actors are able to access the large amounts of personal data that they contain, or the sources of such data.

50. Moreover, there are risks that emerge when AI systems can be reverse-engineered (i.e., when third parties "copy" the machine learning algorithm by replicating a model based on outputs or queries from the original system). In one example, after copying the algorithm, researchers were able to force it to generate examples of the potentially proprietary data from which it learned. If the algorithms are built on personal data, some of that information might become accessible as well.[22]

---

[21] Eykholt, Kevin et al., "Robust Physical-World Attacks on Deep Learning Models", Cornell University Library, 2017, https://arxiv.org/abs/1707.08945

[22] Wired, "How to steal an AI", 2016, https://www.wired.com/2016/09/how-to-steal-an-ai/

Recommendations

General Considerations

51. As declared by the International Conference of Data Protection and Privacy Commissioners[23], Artificial intelligence and machine learning technologies should be designed, developed and used in accordance with the principles of

- fairness and respect of fundamental human rights,

- accountability and vigilance,

- transparency and intelligibility,

- privacy by design and by default,

- empowerment and respect of individual rights, and

- non-discrimination and avoidance of biased decisions.

All stakeholders, including researchers, developers and users of AI systems as well as legislators and regulators, should contribute to ensuring that the further evolution of AI systems is governed by these principles.

52. <u>Fairness and respect of fundamental human rights</u>

Fairness and respect for human rights require that data are used only in a manner consistent with the reasonable expectations of the individuals concerned, and only for purposes compatible with those for which they were collected, taking account of the impact not only on individuals, but also on groups and society as a whole, and ensuring that AI does not endanger human development. In short, there must be boundaries on uses of AI, and AI systems should not reflect unfair bias or make impermissible discriminatory decisions.

53. <u>Accountability and vigilance</u>

---

[23] 40th ICDPPC – Brussels, 2018, Declaration on Ethics and Data Protection in Artificial Intelligence, https://icdppc.org/wp-content/uploads/2018/10/20180922_ICDPPC-40th_AI-Declaration_ADOPTED.pdf; see also Universal Guidelines for Artificial Intelligence (2018), https://thepublicvoice.org/ai-universal-guidelines/

Accountability and vigilance require the establishment of oversight mechanisms for audits, continuous monitoring and impact assessment of artificial intelligence systems, and their periodic review, collective and joint responsibility of all actors and stakeholders, awareness raising, education, research and training, and where necessary the involvement of trusted third parties or independent ethics committees.

54. Organizations, not algorithms, are accountable for the results of all data processing involving the use of AI-based systems or services. To help ensure accountability, roles and responsibilities must be clearly defined, assigned and well documented.

55. In instances where an organization is using an AI-based service provided by a third party, the respective roles, responsibilities and rights of the organization and supplier with respect to the processing of personal data, including those related to the security of the AI systems, should be clearly articulated and allocated.

56. Organizations need to demonstrate that they are being accountable and can make responsible and ethical decisions regarding their use of AI-based services. Both models and their underlying algorithms require continuous assessment. This necessitates regular audits to ensure that decisions resulting from the profiling are responsible, fair, ethical and compatible with the purpose(s) for which the information was collected and is being used.

57. Transparency and intelligibility

Transparency and intelligibility require scientific research on explainable artificial intelligence, the development of innovative ways of communicating relevant information, transparent practices of organizations and of algorithms, auditability of systems, appropriate information to individuals so that they are aware when they interact with AI systems or provide data to them and overarching human control of the systems.

58. AI-based systems and services should be designed to support internal and/or external audit or review. As far as possible, AI-based systems and services should be based on data, algorithms, models, protocols, designs and implementations that are open for external review and/or testing. Open audits, or audits by trusted entities, can help to provide assurance that the AI-based services do in fact have all the claimed properties and will not generate unfair or discriminatory outcomes.

59. Where possible, AI-based systems and services should be based on data, algorithms, models, protocols, designs and implementations that are as intelligible as possible. A number of promising techniques have been proposed including:

- Explainable AI (XAI)[24]: XAI is the idea that all the automated decisions made should be explicable. With people involved in a process, it is often desirable that an explanation is given for the outcome. As an example, there is a project underway in this field, being run by the Defense Advanced Research Projects Agency (DARPA), where the objective is to gain more knowledge about providing understandable explanations for automated decisions;

- Local Interpretable Model-Agnostic Explanations (LIME)[25]: LIME is a solution that produces explanations ordinary people can understand. In the case of image recognition, for example, it will be able to show which parts of the picture are relevant for what it thinks the image is. This makes it easy for anyone to comprehend the basis for a decision; or

- Counterfactual explanations[26]: These are explanations that describe the smallest change to a variable used by the algorithm (like income, test scores, or account activity) that would be needed for the algorithm to arrive at a desirable outcome. As multiple variables or sets of variables can lead to one or more desirable outcomes, multiple counterfactual explanations can be provided, corresponding to different choices of nearby possible worlds for which the counterfactual holds. Counterfactuals describe a dependency on the external facts that lead to that decision without the need to convey the internal state or logic of an algorithm. These explanations thus aim at informing and helping the individual understand why a particular decision was reached, providing grounds to contest the decision if the outcome is undesired, and understanding what would need to change in order to receive a desired result in the future.

---

[24] DARPA, "Explainable Artificial Intelligence (XAI)", https://www.darpa.mil/program/explainable-artificial-intelligence

[25] Tulio Ribeiro, Marco, Singh, Sameer, Guestrin, Carlos, ""Why Should I Trust You?": Explaining the Predictions of Any Classifier", Cornell University, 2016, https://arxiv.org/abs/1602.04938

[26] Wachter, Sandra and Mittelstadt, Brent and Russell, Chris, "Counterfactual Explanations Without Opening the Black Box: Automated Decisions and the GDPR", Harvard Journal of Law & Technology, 31 (2), 2018. SSRN: https://ssrn.com/abstract=3063289 or http://dx.doi.org/10.2139/ssrn.3063289

60. In relation to AI-based systems or services, information regarding the categories of information collected, the purposes for which the information will be used, the identity of the actors involved in the processing, how long the data will be retained and the general security practices that are in place, should be published. This information should be kept up-to-date and should be clearly communicated to relevant individuals.

61. Privacy and Ethics by Design

Privacy and ethics by design and by default require implementing technical and organizational measures and procedures, assessing and documenting the expected impacts on individuals and society and identifying specific requirements for ethical and fair use of the systems and for respecting human rights as part of the development and operations of any artificial intelligence system.

62. AI-based systems and services should be developed and designed in accordance with privacy and ethics by design principles.

63. AI-based systems and services should be subject to an independent ethics review mechanism, either internal or external[27], to ensure that the proposed AI system or service will behave in an ethical manner.

64. AI-based systems and services should be subject to extensive testing to ensure that any regulatory or ethics-related design issues related to the product or service are identified and addressed in a timely manner.

65. AI-based systems and services should be subject to a privacy impact assessment and a risk analysis at appropriate stages of their lifecycle (e.g., development, implementation, decommissioning). The necessary technical and organizational measures, identified during these analyses, should be implemented.

66. Empowerment

---

[27] See, for example, Trilateral Research, "Research ethics for industry 4.0", https://trilateralresearch.co.uk/research-ethics-for-industry-4-0/, or O'Neil Risk Consulting and Algorithmic Auditing (ORCAA), at http://www.oneilrisk.com/ for examples of a commercially available "ethics board".

The opportunities offered by AI should be used to foster equal empowerment and enhance public engagement. This means respecting and facilitating the exercise of individuals' rights to data protection and privacy such as the rights to access to information, to object or request erasure of information, as well as the rights of freedom of expression and information, non-discrimination and, where applicable, individuals' right not to be subject to a decision based solely on automated processing or the individuals' right to challenge such decision.

67. Those who are subject to an automated decision by an AI-based system or service should be informed that they have been subject to such a decision and should have the opportunity to fully understand the reasoning behind that decision as well as the factors that (most) influenced the decision. Any associated automated decision-making or other rule-based systems and the reasoning underlying determinations made with or by those systems must be explainable to individuals and organizational users in clear, simple, and easy to understand language.

68. Non-discrimination

Non-discrimination and the avoidance of biased decisions require recognition of and respect for international legal instruments on human rights, research into technical ways to identify, address and mitigate biases, ensuring that the personal data is accurate, up-to-date and as complete as possible, and specific guidance and principles in addressing biases and discrimination.

69. There may be several forms or stages of training for AI systems (e.g., initial training during development, acceptance testing during implementation, and ongoing training during use). At all stages of an AI-based system and service's lifecycle, steps should be taken to ensure that training data is of the highest quality and relevance possible. This includes ensuring the data is as correct, accurate, complete, relevant, representative and up-to-date as possible. It also includes ensuring that, to the greatest extent possible, the data is free from bias based on race, age, gender, sexual orientation, religious belief, income level, or other protected grounds.

Specific Considerations

Developers (of AI components, systems and services)

70. Developers should ensure that the purposes for which they are processing personal data (e.g., system training to enhance face recognition) are clearly defined, well documented and correspond with the expectations of individuals about the use of their information.

71. Developers should minimize, to the greatest extent possible, the amount of personal data used during development, and ensure that any such data is limited to that which is relevant and necessary for the defined purposes (e.g., training). In addition to techniques such as the use of anonymized data, several possible techniques have been identified that may enable this minimisation including, but not limited to:

- Generative Adversarial Networks (GANs)[28]: GANs are used for generating synthetic data. As of today, GANs have mainly been used for the generation of images. However, it also has the potential for becoming a method for generating huge volumes of high quality, synthetic training data in other areas. This may satisfy the need for both labelled data and large volumes of data, without the need to utilise great amounts of data containing real personal information;

- Federated Machine Learning[29]: This is a form of distributed learning. Federated learning works by downloading the latest version of a centralized model to a client unit, for example a mobile phone. The model is then improved locally on the client unit, on the basis of local data. The changes to the model are then sent back to the server where they are consolidated with the change information from models on other clients. An average of the changed information is then used to improve the centralized model. The new, improved centralized model may now be downloaded by all the clients. This provides an opportunity to improve an existing model, on the basis of a large number of users, without having to share the users' data;

- Transfer Learning[30]: it is not always necessary to develop models from scratch. Existing models that solve similar tasks can be utilized. By basing processing on these existing models, it will often be possible to achieve the same result with less data and in a shorter time. There are libraries containing pre-trained models that can be used; and

---

[28] Ian J. Goodfellow, Jean Pouget-Abadie, Mehdi Mirza, Bing Xu, David Warde-Farley, Sherjil Ozair, Aaron Courville, Yoshua Bengio, "Generative Adversarial Nets", Département d'informatique et de recherche opérationnelle Université de Montréal, https://papers.nips.cc/paper/5423-generative-adversarial-nets.pdf

[29] Google AI Blog, Federated Learning: Collaborative Machine Learning without Centralized Training Data, 2017, https://ai.googleblog.com/2017/04/federated-learning-collaborative.html

[30] Machine Learning Research Group, University of Texas at Austin, http://www.cs.utexas.edu/~ml/publications/area/125/transfer_learning

- Matrix capsules[31]: Matrix capsules are a new variant of neural networks, and require less data for learning than the current norm for deep learning. This is very advantageous because a lot less data is required for machine learning.

72. Where possible, developers should make the training data available for external review and/or testing. Where this is not possible (for instance, if the data is business sensitive), organizations should be able to clearly demonstrate that they have taken steps to ensure the quality and relevance of the data, either internally or through the use of a reputable third party.

Providers (of AI components, systems and services)

73. Providers should ensure their systems include mechanisms and techniques that will support compliance with relevant privacy regulation and document how these requirements are met. Documentation is one of the requirements of the regulations, and may be requested by customers, users or oversight bodies.

74. As appropriate, providers should ensure that data used for marketing and sales purposes, or as part of acceptance testing, is as correct, accurate, relevant, representative, complete and up-to-date as possible.

75. Providers should ensure that their algorithms, data, protocols, designs and implementations are open for external review and/or testing. Open audits, or audits by trusted entities, can help to provide assurance that the AI-based systems or services in fact have all the claimed properties and will not generate unfair or discriminatory outcomes.

Organizations (implementing and using AI systems or services)

76. Organizations intending to use AI-based systems or services should ensure that they have an appropriate legal basis for the processing of personal data.

77. Organizations intending to acquire or use AI-based systems or services should specify their privacy and data protection requirements, as well as any additional requirements (e.g., with respect to transparency, and auditability). These requirements should be clearly documented (e.g., in a contract with an AI developer). Organizations should make these requirements known to providers and developers as appropriate.

---

[31] Hinton, Geoffrey, Sara Sabour and Nicholas Frosst, "Matrix capsules with em routing", Google Brain, Toronto, Canada, 2018, https://openreview.net/pdf?id=HJWLfGWRb

78. Organizations should only engage providers of AI-based systems or services that offer sufficient guarantees that the privacy and data protection rights of individuals are adequately protected and that other requirements are adequately addressed.

79. Organizations should ensure that any data used for ongoing training, testing or evaluation of an AI system or service is as correct, accurate, relevant, representative, complete and up-to-date as possible.

80. Organizations should not collect, use, or disclose personal information in ways that would run counter to the context in which individuals provided that data. Organizations wanting to use the collected data for a purpose different than the original one must assess the compatibility between the original and the new purposes on a case-by-case basis.

81. Organizations should only process as much personal data as they need to complete specified purposes. Organizations should minimize the amount of personal data used by the system or service. This minimisation may be achieved through a number of techniques (e.g., removal of the personal data from the data set, using synthetic data instead of actual data, anonymization and so on).

82. Organizations should ensure appropriate transparency regarding the use of algorithms and profiles that may influence decision-making. Any associated automated decision-making or other rule-based systems and the reasoning underlying the determinations made with those systems must be explained to individuals and organizational users in a clear, simple, easy to understand and timely manner.

83. In cases of automated individual decisions, individuals should know the decision was automated, and have access to the decision and its reasoning in order to assess whether their information has been processed fairly. Organizations should implement innovative, practical and expedient procedures that facilitate a human evaluation of decisions in cases where a different point of view is submitted, counter-arguments are presented, or where the decisions are challenged.

Data Protection Authorities

84. Data Protection Authorities (DPAs) should ensure that they possess sufficient knowledge and expertise in order to give guidance and to investigate possible breaches of relevant data protection or privacy regulation. This may be achieved through the acquisition of expertise by DPA staff or by ensuring access to relevant external expertise through partnerships with academia, industry, NGOs and other government agencies as appropriate.

85. DPAs should strengthen their awareness raising activities by providing guidance to relevant stakeholders. This could include promoting the application of privacy by design principles with AI-based services developers, providers and users.

86. DPAs should support the implementation of codes of conduct, data protection and privacy certification schemes, as well as the development of suitable data protection and privacy impact assessment frameworks and tools, in order to foster the development of privacy friendly AI-based systems and services.

87. DPAs should also strengthen their supervisory activities. This could include supporting the development of international arrangements for enforcement cooperation and the conduct of joint enforcement activities. It could also include auditing the development, implementation and use of AI systems and services in order to identify practices that create risks for individuals. As appropriate, DPAs should share the results of these audits with other regulatory authorities.

International Conference of Data Protection and Privacy Commissioners, Declaration on Ethics and Data Protection in Artificial Intelligence (2018)

AUTHORS:

• Commission Nationale de l'Informatique et des Libertés (CNIL), France

• European Data Protection Supervisor (EDPS), European Union

• Garante per la protezione dei dati personali, Italy

CO-SPONSORS:

• Agencia de Acceso a la Información Pública, Argentina

• Commission d'accès à l'information, Québec, Canada

• Datatilsynet (Data Inspectorate), Norway

• Information Commissioner's Office (ICO), United Kingdom

• Préposé fédéral à la protection des données et à la transparence, Switzerland

• Data protection Authority, Belgium

• Privacy Commissioner for Personal Data, Hong-Kong

• Data protection Commission, Ireland

• Data Protection Office, Poland

• Instituto Nacional de Transparencia, Acceso a la Información y Protección de Datos Personales (INAI), Mexico

• National Authority for Data Protection and Freedom of Information, Hungary

• Federal Commissioner for Data Protection and Freedom of Information, Germany

• Office of the Privacy Commissioner (OPC), Canada

• National Privacy Commission, Philippines

The 40th International Conference of Data Protection and Privacy Commissioners:

Considering the initial discussion at the 38th International Conference of Data Protection and Privacy Commissioners in Marrakesh on Artificial intelligence, Robotics, Privacy and Data Protection;

Recognizing that artificial intelligence systems may bring significant benefits for users and society, including by: increasing the rapidity of processes and supporting decision-making; creating new ways to participate in democratic processes; improving efficiency in public sector and industry; achieving more equitable distribution of resources and opportunities; offering new methods and solutions in various fields such as public health, medical care, security, sustainable development, agriculture and transport; bringing new opportunities in scientific research and education and; providing individuals with more personalized services;

Taking into account the significant progress in certain areas of artificial intelligence, in particular regarding the processing of large amounts of information, the analysis and prediction of human behavior and characteristics, and in related fields such as robotics, computer vision and autonomous systems, likely to make significant progress in the near future;

Highlighting the rapid advancement of big data and artificial intelligence, notably machine learning, in particular with the development of deep learning technologies, allowing algorithms to solve complex operations leading to potential decisions, making however such processes more opaque;

Affirming that the respect of the rights to privacy and data protection are increasingly challenged by the development of artificial intelligence and that this development should be complemented by ethical and human rights considerations;

Considering that machine learning technologies in particular, and artificial intelligence systems in general, may rely on the processing of large sets of personal data for their development, potentially impacting data protection and privacy; also taking into account the potential risks induced by the current trend of market concentration in the field of artificial intelligence;

Recognizing the link between collections, uses and disclosures of personal information – the traditional sphere of privacy and data protection – on the one hand, and the direct impacts on human rights more broadly, most notably regarding discrimination and freedom of expression and information, and thus acknowledging the need for data protection and privacy authorities to think about human rights more broadly, and for data protection and privacy authorities to work with other authorities addressing human rights;

Pointing out that some data sets used to train machine learning-based and artificial intelligence systems have been found to contain inherent bias resulting in decisions which can unfairly discriminate against certain individuals or groups, potentially restricting the availability of certain services or content, and thus interfering with individuals' rights such as freedom of expression and information or resulting in the exclusion of people from certain aspects of personal, social, professional life;

Stressing that artificial intelligence powered systems whose decisions cannot be explained raise fundamental questions of accountability not only for privacy and data protection law but also liability in the event of errors and harm;

Noting that many stakeholders in the field of artificial intelligence have expressed their concerns about the risks of malicious use of artificial intelligence, as well as the risks related to privacy, data protection and human dignity, pointing out for example that the development of artificial intelligence in combination with mass surveillance raises concerns about their possible use to curtail fundamental rights and freedoms;

Highlighting that those risks and challenges may affect individuals and society, and that the extent and nature of potential consequences are currently uncertain;

Emphasising the importance of trust, since strong data protection and privacy safeguards help to build individuals' trust in how their data is processed, which encourages data sharing and thereby promotes innovation;

Taking the view that the current challenges triggered by the development of artificial intelligence and machine learning systems reinforce the need for the adoption of an international approach and standards, in order to ensure the promotion and protection of human rights in all digital developments at international level;

Reaffirming the commitment of data protection authorities and the Conference of Data Protection and Privacy Commissioners to uphold data protection and privacy principles in adapting to this evolving environment, notably by engaging resources and developing new skills in order to be prepared for future changes.

The **40th International Conference of Data Protection and Privacy Commissioners** considers that any creation, development and use of artificial intelligence systems shall fully respect human rights, particularly the rights to the protection of personal data and to privacy, as well as human dignity, non-discrimination and fundamental values, and shall provide solutions to allow individuals to maintain control and understanding of artificial intelligence systems.

The Conference therefore endorses the following guiding principles, as its core values to preserve human rights in the development of artificial intelligence:

1. Artificial intelligence and machine learning technologies should be designed, developed and used in respect of fundamental human rights and in accordance with the **fairness principle**, in particular by:

> a. Considering individuals' reasonable expectations by ensuring that the use of artificial intelligence systems remains consistent with their original purposes, and that the data are used in a way that is not incompatible with the original purpose of their collection,

> b. taking into consideration not only the impact that the use of artificial intelligence may have on the individual, but also the collective impact on groups and on society at large,

> c. ensuring that artificial intelligence systems are developed in a way that facilitates human development and does not obstruct or endanger it, thus recognizing the need for delineation and boundaries on certain uses,

2. **Continued attention and vigilance,** as well as accountability, for the potential effects and consequences of, artificial intelligence systems should be ensured, in particular by:

> a. promoting accountability of all relevant stakeholders to individuals, supervisory authorities and other third parties as appropriate, including through the realization of audit, continuous monitoring and impact assessment of artificial intelligence systems, and periodic review of oversight mechanisms;

> b. fostering collective and joint responsibility, involving the whole chain of actors and stakeholders, for example with the development of collaborative standards and the sharing of best practices,

c. investing in awareness raising, education, research and training in order to ensure a good level of information on and understanding of artificial intelligence and its potential effects in society, and

d. establishing demonstrable governance processes for all relevant actors, such as relying on trusted third parties or the setting up of independent ethics committees,

3. Artificial intelligence **systems transparency and intelligibility** should be improved, with the objective of effective implementation, in particular by:

a. investing in public and private scientific research on explainable artificial intelligence,

b. promoting transparency, intelligibility and reachability, for instance through the development of innovative ways of communication, taking into account the different levels of transparency and information required for each relevant audience,

c. making organizations' practices more transparent, notably by promoting algorithmic transparency and the auditability of systems, while ensuring meaningfulness of the information provided, and

d. guaranteeing the right to informational self-determination, notably by ensuring that individuals are always informed appropriately when they are interacting directly with an artificial intelligence system or when they provide personal data to be processed by such systems,

e. providing adequate information on the purpose and effects of artificial intelligence systems in order to verify continuous alignment with expectation of individuals and to enable overall human control on such systems.

4. As part of an overall "ethics by design" approach, artificial intelligence systems should be **designed and developed responsibly**, by applying the principles of **privacy by default and privacy by design**, in particular by:

a. implementing technical and organizational measures and procedures – proportional to the type of system that is developed – to ensure that data subjects' privacy and personal data are respected, both when determining the means of the processing and at the moment of data processing,

b. assessing and documenting the expected impacts on individuals and society at the beginning of an artificial intelligence project and for relevant developments during its entire life cycle, and

c. identifying specific requirements for ethical and fair use of the systems and for respecting human rights as part of the development and operations of any artificial intelligence system,

5. **Empowerment of every individual** should be promoted, and the exercise of individuals' rights should be encouraged, as well as the creation of opportunities for public engagement, in particular by:

a. respecting data protection and privacy rights, including where applicable the right to information, the right to access, the right to object to processing and the right to erasure, and promoting those rights through education and awareness campaigns,

b. respecting related rights including freedom of expression and information, as well as non-discrimination,

c. recognizing that the right to object or appeal applies to technologies that influence personal development or opinions and guaranteeing, where applicable, individuals' right not to be subject to a decision based solely on automated processing if it significantly affects them and, where not applicable, guaranteeing individuals' right to challenge such decision,

d. using the capabilities of artificial intelligence systems to foster an equal empowerment and enhance public engagement, for example through adaptable interfaces and accessible tools.

6. Unlawful **biases or discriminations** that may result from the use of data in artificial intelligence should be reduced and mitigated, including by:

a. ensuring the respect of international legal instruments on human rights and non-discrimination,

b. investing in research into technical ways to identify, address and mitigate biases,

c. taking reasonable steps to ensure the personal data and information used in automated decision making is accurate, up-to-date and as complete as possible, and

d. elaborating specific guidance and principles in addressing biases and discrimination, and promoting individuals' and stakeholders' awareness.

Taking into consideration the principles above, the 40th International Conference of Data Protection and Privacy Commissioners calls for **common governance principles on artificial intelligence** to be established, fostering concerted international efforts in this field, in order to ensure that its development and use take place in accordance with ethics and human values, and respect human dignity. These common governance principles must be able to tackle the challenges raised by the rapid evolutions of artificial intelligence technologies, on the basis of a multi-stakeholder approach in order to address all cross-sectoral issues at stake. They must take place at an international level since the development of artificial intelligence is a trans-border phenomenon and may affect all humanity. The Conference should be involved in this international effort, working with and supporting general and sectoral authorities in other fields such as competition, market and consumer regulation.

The 40th International Conference of Data Protection and Privacy Commissioners therefore establishes, as a contribution to a future common governance at the international level, and in order to further elaborate guidance to accompany the principles on Ethics and Data Protection in Artificial Intelligence, a **permanent working group** addressing the challenges of artificial intelligence development. This **working group on Ethics and Data Protection in Artificial Intelligence** will be in charge of promoting understanding of and respect for

European Commission, High Level Expert Group on Artificial Intelligence, Ethics Guidelines for Trustworthy AI
(2019)
(footnotes not included)

EXECUTIVE SUMMARY

The aim of the Guidelines is to promote Trustworthy AI. Trustworthy AI has **three components**, which should be met throughout the system's entire life cycle: (1) it should be **lawful**, complying with all applicable laws and regulations (2) it should be **ethical**, ensuring adherence to ethical principles and values and (3) it should be **robust**, both from a technical and social perspective since, even with good intentions, AI systems can cause unintentional harm. Each component in itself is necessary but not sufficient for the achievement of Trustworthy AI. Ideally, all three components work in harmony and overlap in their operation. If, in practice, tensions arise between these components, society should endeavour to align them.

These Guidelines set out a **framework for achieving Trustworthy AI.** The framework does not explicitly deal with Trustworthy AI's first component (lawful AI). Instead, it aims to offer guidance on the second and third components: fostering and securing ethical and robust AI. Addressed to all stakeholders, these Guidelines seek to go beyond a list of ethical principles, by providing guidance on how such principles can be operationalised in socio-technical systems. Guidance is provided in three layers of abstraction, from the most abstract in Chapter I to the most concrete in Chapter III, closing with examples of opportunities and critical concerns raised by AI systems.

I. Based on an approach founded on fundamental rights, **Chapter I** identifies the **ethical principles** and their correlated values that must be respected in the development, deployment and use of AI systems.

...

II. Drawing upon Chapter I, **Chapter II** provides guidance on how Trustworthy AI can be realised, by listing **seven requirements** that AI systems should meet. Both technical and non-technical methods can be used for their implementation.

...

III. Chapter III provides a concrete and non-exhaustive Trustworthy AI assessment list aimed at operationalising the key requirements set out in Chapter II.

This **assessment list** will need to be tailored to the specific use case of the AI system.

...

A final section of the document aims to concretise some of the issues touched upon throughout the framework, by offering examples of beneficial opportunities that should be pursued, and critical concerns raised by AI systems that should be carefully considered.

While these Guidelines aim to offer guidance for AI applications in general by building a horizontal foundation to achieve Trustworthy AI, different situations raise different challenges. It should therefore be explored whether, in addition to this horizontal framework, a sectorial approach is needed, given the context-specificity of AI systems.

These Guidelines do not intend to substitute any form of current or future policymaking or regulation, nor do they aim to deter the introduction thereof. They should be seen as a living document to be reviewed and updated over time to ensure their continuous relevance as the technology, our social environments, and our knowledge evolve. This document is a starting point for the discussion about "Trustworthy AI for Europe".

Beyond Europe, the Guidelines also aim to foster research, reflection and discussion on an ethical framework for AI systems at a global level.

...

Chapter I: Foundations of Trustworthy AI

This Chapter sets out the foundations of Trustworthy AI, grounded in fundamental rights and reflected by four ethical principles that should be adhered to in order to ensure ethical and robust AI. It draws heavily on the field of ethics.

AI ethics is a sub-field of applied ethics, focusing on the ethical issues raised by the development, deployment and use of AI. Its central concern is to identify how AI can advance or raise concerns to the good life of individuals, whether in terms of quality of life, or human autonomy and freedom necessary for a democratic society.

Ethical reflection on AI technology can serve multiple purposes. First, it can stimulate reflection on the need to protect individuals and groups at the most basic level. Second, it can stimulate new kinds of innovations that seek to foster ethical values, such as those helping to achieve the UN Sustainable Development Goals13, which are firmly embedded in the forthcoming EU Agenda 2030. While this document mostly concerns itself with the first purpose mentioned, the importance that ethics could have in the second should not be underestimated. Trustworthy AI can improve individual flourishing and collective wellbeing by generating prosperity, value creation and wealth maximization. It can contribute to achieving a fair society, by helping to increase citizens' health and well-being in ways that foster equality in the distribution of economic, social and political opportunity.

It is therefore imperative that we understand how to best support AI development, deployment and use to ensure that everyone can thrive in an AI-based world, and to build a better future while at the same time being globally competitive. As with any powerful technology, the use of AI systems in our society raises several ethical challenges, for instance relating to their impact on people and society, decision-making capabilities and safety. If we are increasingly going to use the assistance of or delegate decisions to AI systems, we need to make sure these systems are fair in their impact on people's lives, that they are in line with values that should not be compromised and able to act accordingly, and that suitable accountability processes can ensure this.

Europe needs to define what normative vision of an AI-immersed future it wants to realise, and understand which notion of AI should be studied, developed, deployed and used in Europe to achieve this vision. With this document, we intend to contribute to this effort by introducing the notion of Trustworthy AI, which we believe is the right way to build a future with AI. A future where democracy, the rule of law and fundamental rights underpin AI systems and where such systems continuously improve and defend democratic culture will also enable an environment where innovation and responsible competitiveness can thrive.

A domain-specific ethics code – however consistent, developed and fine-grained future versions of it may be – can never function as a substitute for ethical reasoning itself, which must always remain sensitive to contextual details that cannot be captured in general Guidelines. Beyond developing a set of rules, ensuring Trustworthy AI requires us to build and maintain an ethical culture and mind-set through public debate, education and practical learning.

1. Fundamental rights as moral and legal entitlements

We believe in an approach to AI ethics based on the fundamental rights enshrined in the EU Treaties, the EU Charter and international human rights law. Respect for fundamental rights, within a framework of democracy and the rule of law, provides the most promising foundations for identifying abstract ethical principles and values, which can be operationalised in the context of AI.

The EU Treaties and the EU Charter prescribe a series of fundamental rights that EU member states and EU institutions are legally obliged to respect when implementing EU law. These rights are described in the EU Charter by reference to dignity, freedoms, equality and solidarity, citizens' rights and justice. The common foundation that unites these rights can be understood as rooted in respect for human dignity – thereby reflecting what we describe as a "human-centric approach" in which the human being enjoys a unique and inalienable moral status of primacy in the civil, political, economic and social fields.

While the rights set out in the EU Charter are legally binding, it is important to recognise that fundamental rights do not provide comprehensive legal protection in every case. For the EU Charter, for instance, it is important to underline that its field of application is limited to areas of EU law. International human rights law and in particular the European Convention on Human Rights are legally binding on EU Member States, including in areas that fall outside the scope of EU law. At the same time, fundamental rights are also bestowed on individuals and (to a certain degree) groups by virtue of their moral status as human beings, independently of their legal force. Understood as legally enforceable rights, fundamental rights therefore fall under the first component of Trustworthy AI (lawful AI), which safeguards compliance with the law. Understood as the rights of everyone, rooted in the inherent moral status of human beings, they also underpin the second component of Trustworthy AI (ethical AI), dealing with ethical norms that are not necessarily legally binding yet crucial to ensure trustworthiness. Since this document does not aim to offer guidance on the former component, for the purpose of these non-binding guidelines, references to fundamental rights reflect the latter component.

2. From fundamental rights to ethical principles

2.1 Fundamental rights as a basis for Trustworthy AI

Among the comprehensive set of indivisible rights set out in international human rights law, the EU Treaties and the EU Charter, the below families of fundamental rights are particularly apt to cover AI systems. Many of these rights are, in specified circumstances, legally enforceable in the EU so that compliance with their terms is legally obligatory. But even after compliance with legally enforceable fundamental rights has been achieved, ethical reflection can help us understand how the development, deployment and use of AI systems may implicate fundamental rights and their underlying values, and can help provide more fine-grained guidance when seeking to identify what we *should* do rather than what we (currently) *can* do with technology.

Respect for human dignity. Human dignity encompasses the idea that every human being possesses an "intrinsic worth", which should never be diminished, compromised or repressed by others – nor by new technologies like AI systems. In this context, respect for human dignity entails that all people are treated with respect due to them as moral *subjects*, rather than merely as *objects* to be sifted, sorted, scored, herded, conditioned or manipulated. AI systems should hence be developed in a manner that respects, serves and protects humans' physical and mental integrity, personal and cultural sense of identity, and satisfaction of their essential needs.

Freedom of the individual. Human beings should remain free to make life decisions for themselves. This entails freedom from sovereign intrusion, but also requires intervention from government and non-governmental organisations to ensure that individuals or people at risk of exclusion have equal access to AI's benefits and opportunities. In an AI context, freedom of the individual for instance requires mitigation of (in)direct illegitimate coercion, threats to mental autonomy and mental health, unjustified surveillance, deception and unfair manipulation. In fact, freedom of the individual means a commitment to enabling individuals to wield even higher control over their lives, including (among other rights) protection of the freedom to conduct a business, the freedom of the arts and science, freedom of expression, the right to private life and privacy, and freedom of assembly and association.

Respect for democracy, justice and the rule of law. All governmental power in constitutional democracies must be legally authorised and limited by law. AI systems should serve to maintain and foster democratic processes and respect the plurality of values and life choices of individuals. AI systems must not undermine democratic processes, human deliberation or democratic voting systems. AI systems must also embed a commitment to ensure that they do not operate in ways that undermine the foundational commitments upon which the rule of law is founded, mandatory laws and regulation, and to ensure due process and equality before the law.

Equality, non-discrimination and solidarity - *including the rights of persons at risk of exclusion*. Equal respect for the moral worth and dignity of all human beings must be ensured. This goes beyond non-discrimination, which tolerates the drawing of distinctions between dissimilar situations based on objective justifications. In an AI context, equality entails that the system's operations cannot generate unfairly biased outputs (e.g. the data used to train AI systems should be as inclusive as possible, representing different population groups). This also requires adequate respect for potentially vulnerable persons and groups, such as workers, women, persons with disabilities, ethnic minorities, children, consumers or others at risk of exclusion.

Citizens' rights*.* Citizens benefit from a wide array of rights, including the right to vote, the right to good administration or access to public documents, and the right to petition the administration. AI systems offer substantial potential to improve the scale and efficiency of government in the provision of public goods and services to society. At the same time, citizens' rights could also be negatively impacted by AI systems and should be safeguarded. When the term "citizens' rights" is used here, this is not to deny or neglect the rights of third-country nationals and irregular (or illegal) persons in the EU who also have rights under international law, and – therefore – in the area of AI systems.

2.2 Ethical Principles in the Context of AI Systems

Many public, private, and civil organizations have drawn inspiration from fundamental rights to produce ethical frameworks for AI systems. In the EU, the European Group on Ethics in Science and New Technologies ("EGE") proposed a set of 9 basic principles, based on the fundamental values laid down in the EU Treaties and Charter. We build further on this work, recognising most of the principles hitherto propounded by various groups, while clarifying the ends that all principles seek to nurture and support. These ethical principles can inspire new and specific regulatory instruments, can help interpreting fundamental rights as our socio-technical environment evolves over time, and can guide the rationale for AI systems' development, deployment and use – adapting dynamically as society itself evolves.

AI systems should improve individual and collective wellbeing. This section lists **four ethical principles**, rooted in fundamental rights, which must be respected in order to ensure that AI systems are developed, deployed and used in a trustworthy manner. They are specified as **ethical imperatives**, such that AI practitioners should always strive to adhere to them. Without imposing a hierarchy, we list the principles here below in manner that mirrors the order of appearance of the fundamental rights upon which they are based in the EU Charter.

These are the principles of:

> (i) Respect for human autonomy

> (ii) Prevention of harm

> (iii) Fairness

> (iv) Explicability

Many of these are to a large extent already reflected in existing legal requirements for which mandatory compliance is required and hence also fall within the scope of lawful AI, which is Trustworthy AI's first component. Yet, as set out above, while many legal obligations reflect ethical principles, adherence to ethical principles goes beyond formal compliance with existing laws.

■ *The principle of respect for human autonomy*

The fundamental rights upon which the EU is founded are directed towards ensuring respect for the freedom and autonomy of human beings. Humans interacting with AI systems must be able to keep full and effective self-determination over themselves, and be able to partake in the democratic process. AI systems should not unjustifiably subordinate, coerce, deceive, manipulate, condition or herd humans. Instead, they should be designed to augment, complement and empower human cognitive, social and cultural skills. The allocation of functions between humans and AI systems should follow human-centric design principles and leave meaningful opportunity for human choice. This means securing human oversight over work processes in AI systems. AI systems may also fundamentally change the work sphere. It should support humans in the working environment, and aim for the creation of meaningful work.

■ *The principle of prevention of harm*

AI systems should neither cause nor exacerbate harm or otherwise adversely affect human beings. This entails the protection of human dignity as well as mental and physical integrity. AI systems and the environments in which they operate must be safe and secure. They must be technically robust and it should be ensured that they are not open to malicious use. Vulnerable persons should receive greater attention and be included in the development, deployment and use of AI systems. Particular attention must also be paid to situations where AI systems can cause or exacerbate adverse impacts due to asymmetries of power or information, such as between employers and employees, businesses and consumers or governments and citizens. Preventing harm also entails consideration of the natural environment and all living beings.

■ *The principle of fairness*

The development, deployment and use of AI systems must be fair. While we acknowledge that there are many different interpretations of fairness, we believe that fairness has both a substantive and a procedural dimension. The substantive dimension implies a commitment to: ensuring equal and just distribution of both benefits and costs, and ensuring that individuals and groups are free from unfair bias, discrimination and stigmatisation. If unfair biases can be avoided, AI systems could even increase societal fairness. Equal opportunity in terms of access to education, goods, services and technology should also be fostered. Moreover, the use of AI systems should never lead to people being deceived or unjustifiably impaired in their freedom of choice. Additionally, fairness implies that AI practitioners should respect the principle of proportionality between means and ends, and consider carefully how to balance competing interests and objectives. The procedural dimension of fairness entails the ability to contest and seek effective redress against decisions made by AI systems and by the humans operating them. In order to do so, the entity accountable for the decision must be identifiable, and the decision-making processes should be explicable.

■ *The principle of explicability*

Explicability is crucial for building and maintaining users' trust in AI systems. This means that processes need to be transparent, the capabilities and purpose of AI systems openly communicated, and decisions – to the extent possible – explainable to those directly and indirectly affected. Without such information, a decision cannot be duly contested. An explanation as to why a model has generated a particular output or decision (and what combination of input factors contributed to that) is not always possible. These cases are referred to as 'black box' algorithms and require special attention. In those circumstances, other explicability measures (e.g. traceability, auditability and transparent communication on system capabilities) may be required, provided that the system as a whole respects fundamental rights. The degree to which explicability is needed is highly dependent on the context and the severity of the consequences if that output is erroneous or otherwise inaccurate.

2.3 Tensions between the principles

Tensions may arise between the above principles, for which there is no fixed solution. In line with the EU fundamental commitment to democratic engagement, due process and open political participation, methods of accountable deliberation to deal with such tensions should be established. For instance, in various application domains, *the principle of prevention of harm* and *the principle of human autonomy* may be in conflict. Consider as an example the use of AI systems for 'predictive policing', which may help to reduce crime, but in ways that entail surveillance activities that impinge on individual liberty and privacy. Furthermore, AI systems' overall benefits should substantially exceed the foreseeable individual risks. While the above principles certainly offer guidance towards solutions, they remain abstract ethical prescriptions. AI practitioners can hence not be expected to find the right solution based on the principles above, yet they should approach ethical dilemmas and trade-offs via reasoned, evidence-based reflection rather than intuition or random discretion.

There may be situations, however, where no ethically acceptable trade-offs can be identified. Certain fundamental rights and correlated principles are absolute and cannot be subject to a balancing exercise (e.g. human dignity).

...

Chapter II: Realising Trustworthy AI

This Chapter offers guidance on the implementation and realisation of Trustworthy AI, via a list of seven requirements that should be met, building on the principles outlined in Chapter I. In addition, available technical and non-technical methods are introduced for the implementation of these requirements throughout the AI system's life cycle.

1. Requirements of Trustworthy AI

The principles outlined in Chapter I must be translated into concrete requirements to achieve Trustworthy AI. These requirements are applicable to different stakeholders partaking in AI systems' life cycle: developers, deployers and end-users, as well as the broader society. By developers, we refer to those who research, design and/or develop AI systems. By deployers, we refer to public or private organisations that use AI systems within their business processes and to offer products and services to others. End-users are those engaging with the AI system, directly or indirectly. Finally, the broader society encompasses all others that are directly or indirectly affected by AI systems.

Different groups of stakeholders have different roles to play in ensuring that the requirements are met:

> a. Developers should implement and apply the requirements to design and development processes;
>
> b. Deployers should ensure that the systems they use and the products and services they offer meet the requirements;
>
> c. End-users and the broader society should be informed about these requirements and able to request that they are upheld.

The below list of requirements is non-exhaustive. It includes systemic, individual and societal aspects:

1 Human agency and oversight

Including fundamental rights, human agency and human oversight

2 Technical robustness and safety

Including resilience to attack and security, fall back plan and general safety, accuracy, reliability and reproducibility

3 Privacy and data governance

Including respect for privacy, quality and integrity of data, and access to data

4 Transparency

Including traceability, explainability and communication

5 Diversity, non-discrimination and fairness

Including the avoidance of unfair bias, accessibility and universal design, and stakeholder participation

6 Societal and environmental wellbeing

Including sustainability and environmental friendliness, social impact, society and democracy

7 Accountability

Including auditability, minimisation and reporting of negative impact, trade-offs and redress.

...

While all requirements are of equal importance, context and potential tensions between them will need to be taken into account when applying them across different domains and industries. Implementation of these requirements should occur throughout an AI system's entire life cycle and depends on the specific application. While most requirements apply to all AI systems, special attention is given to those directly or indirectly affecting individuals. Therefore, for some applications (for instance in industrial settings), they may be of lesser relevance.

The above requirements include elements that are in some cases already reflected in existing laws. We reiterate that – in line with Trustworthy AI's first component – it is the responsibility of AI practitioners to ensure that they comply with their legal obligations, both as regards horizontally applicable rules as well as domain-specific regulation.

In the following paragraphs, each requirement is explained in more detail.

1.1 Human agency and oversight

AI systems should support human autonomy and decision-making, as prescribed by the principle of *respect for human autonomy*. This requires that AI systems should both act as enablers to a democratic, flourishing and equitable society by supporting the user's agency and foster fundamental rights, and allow for human oversight.

Fundamental rights. Like many technologies, AI systems can equally enable and hamper fundamental rights. They can benefit people for instance by helping them track their personal data, or by increasing the accessibility of education, hence supporting their right to education. However, given the reach and capacity of AI systems, they can also negatively affect fundamental rights. In situations where such risks exist, a fundamental rights impact assessment should be undertaken. This should be done prior to the system's development and include an evaluation of whether those risks can be reduced or justified as necessary in a democratic society in order to respect the rights and freedoms of others. Moreover, mechanisms should be put into place to receive external feedback regarding AI systems that potentially infringe on fundamental rights.

Human agency. Users should be able to make informed autonomous decisions regarding AI systems. They should be given the knowledge and tools to comprehend and interact with AI systems to a satisfactory degree and, where possible, be enabled to reasonably self-assess or challenge the system. AI systems should support individuals in making better, more informed choices in accordance with their goals. AI systems can sometimes be deployed to shape and influence human behaviour through mechanisms that may be difficult to detect, since they may harness sub-conscious processes, including various forms of unfair manipulation, deception, herding and conditioning, all of which may threaten individual autonomy. The overall principle of user autonomy must be central to the system's functionality. Key to this is the right not to be subject to a decision based solely on automated processing when this produces legal effects on users or similarly significantly affects them.

Human oversight. Human oversight helps ensuring that an AI system does not undermine human autonomy or causes other adverse effects. Oversight may be achieved through governance mechanisms such as a human-in-the-loop (HITL), human-on-the-loop (HOTL), or human-in-command (HIC) approach. HITL refers to the capability for human intervention in every decision cycle of the system, which in many cases is neither possible nor desirable. HOTL refers to the capability for human intervention during the design cycle of the system and monitoring the system's operation. HIC refers to the capability to oversee the overall activity of the

AI system (including its broader economic, societal, legal and ethical impact) and the ability to decide when and how to use the system in any particular situation. This can include the decision not to use an AI system in a particular situation, to establish levels of human discretion during the use of the system, or to ensure the ability to override a decision made by a system. Moreover, it must be ensured that public enforcers have the ability to exercise oversight in line with their mandate. Oversight mechanisms can be required in varying degrees to support other safety and control measures, depending on the AI system's application area and potential risk. All other things being equal, the less oversight a human can exercise over an AI system, the more extensive testing and stricter governance is required.

1.2 Technical robustness and safety

A crucial component of achieving Trustworthy AI is technical robustness, which is closely linked to the *principle of prevention of harm*. Technical robustness requires that AI systems be developed with a preventative approach to risks and in a manner such that they reliably behave as intended while minimising unintentional and unexpected harm, and preventing unacceptable harm. This should also apply to potential changes in their operating environment or the presence of other agents (human and artificial) that may interact with the system in an adversarial manner. In addition, the physical and mental integrity of humans should be ensured.

Resilience to attack and security. AI systems, like all software systems, should be protected against vulnerabilities that can allow them to be exploited by adversaries, e.g. hacking. Attacks may target the data (data poisoning), the model (model leakage) or the underlying infrastructure, both software and hardware. If an AI system is attacked, e.g. in adversarial attacks, the data as well as system behaviour can be changed, leading the system to make different decisions, or causing it to shut down altogether. Systems and data can also become corrupted by malicious intention or by exposure to unexpected situations. Insufficient security processes can also result in erroneous decisions or even physical harm. For AI systems to be considered secure, possible unintended applications of the AI system (e.g. dual-use applications) and potential abuse of the system by malicious actors should be taken into account, and steps should be taken to prevent and mitigate these.

Fallback plan and general safety. AI systems should have safeguards that enable a fallback plan in case of problems. This can mean that AI systems switch from a statistical to rule-based procedure, or that they ask for a human operator before continuing their action. It must be ensured that the system will do what it is supposed to do without harming living beings or the environment. This includes the minimisation of unintended consequences and errors. In addition, processes to clarify and assess potential risks associated with the use of AI systems, across various application areas, should be established. The level of safety measures required depends on the magnitude of the risk posed by an AI system, which in turn depends on the system's capabilities. Where it can be foreseen that the development process or the system itself will pose particularly high risks, it is crucial for safety measures to be developed and tested proactively.

Accuracy. Accuracy pertains to an AI system's ability to make correct judgements, for example to correctly classify information into the proper categories, or its ability to make correct predictions, recommendations, or decisions based on data or models. An explicit and well-formed development and evaluation process can support, mitigate and correct unintended risks from inaccurate predictions. When occasional inaccurate predictions cannot be avoided, it is important that the system can indicate how likely these errors are. A high level of accuracy is especially crucial in situations where the AI system directly affects human lives.

Reliability and Reproducibility. It is critical that the results of AI systems are reproducible, as well as reliable. A reliable AI system is one that works properly with a range of inputs and in a range of situations. This is needed to scrutinise an AI system and to prevent unintended harms. Reproducibility describes whether an AI experiment exhibits the same behaviour when repeated under the same conditions. This enables scientists and policy makers to accurately describe what AI systems do. Replication files can facilitate the process of testing and reproducing behaviours.

1.3 Privacy and data governance

Closely linked to the *principle of prevention of harm* is privacy, a fundamental right particularly affected by AI systems. Prevention of harm to privacy also necessitates adequate data governance that covers the quality and integrity of the data used, its relevance in light of the domain in which the AI systems will be deployed, its access protocols and the capability to process data in a manner that protects privacy.

Privacy and data protection. AI systems must guarantee privacy and data protection throughout a system's entire lifecycle. This includes the information initially provided by the user, as well as the information generated about the user over the course of their interaction with the system (e.g. outputs that the AI system generated for specific users or how users responded to particular recommendations). Digital records of human behaviour may allow AI systems to infer not only individuals' preferences, but also their sexual orientation, age, gender, religious or political views. To allow individuals to trust the data gathering process, it must be ensured that data collected about them will not be used to unlawfully or unfairly discriminate against them.

Quality and integrity of data. The quality of the data sets used is paramount to the performance of AI systems. When data is gathered, it may contain socially constructed biases, inaccuracies, errors and mistakes. This needs to be addressed prior to training with any given data set. In addition, the integrity of the data must be ensured. Feeding malicious data into an AI system may change its behaviour, particularly with self-learning systems. Processes and data sets used must be tested and documented at each step such as planning, training, testing and deployment. This should also apply to AI systems that were not developed in-house but acquired elsewhere.

Access to data. In any given organisation that handles individuals' data (whether someone is a user of the system or not), data protocols governing data access should be put in place. These protocols should outline who can access data and under which circumstances. Only duly qualified personnel with the competence and need to access individual's data should be allowed to do so.

1.4 Transparency

This requirement is closely linked with the *principle of explicability* and encompasses transparency of elements relevant to an AI system: the data, the system and the business models.

Traceability. The data sets and the processes that yield the AI system's decision, including those of data gathering and data labelling as well as the algorithms used, should be documented to the best possible standard to allow for traceability and an increase in transparency. This also applies to the decisions made by the AI system. This enables identification of the reasons why an AI-decision was erroneous which, in turn, could help prevent future mistakes. Traceability facilitates auditability as well as explainability.

Explainability. Explainability concerns the ability to explain both the technical processes of an AI system and the related human decisions (e.g. application areas of a system). Technical explainability requires that the decisions made by an AI system can be understood and traced by human beings. Moreover, trade-offs might have to be made between enhancing a system's explainability (which may reduce its accuracy) or increasing its accuracy (at the cost of explainability). Whenever an AI system has a significant impact on people's lives, it should be possible to demand a suitable explanation of the AI system's decision-making process. Such explanation should be timely and adapted to the expertise of the stakeholder concerned (e.g. layperson, regulator or researcher). In addition, explanations of the degree to which an AI system influences and shapes the organisational decision-making process, design choices of the system, and the rationale for deploying it, should be available (hence ensuring business model transparency).

Communication. AI systems should not represent themselves as humans to users; humans have the right to be informed that they are interacting with an AI system. This entails that AI systems must be identifiable as such. In addition, the option to decide against this interaction in favour of human interaction should be provided where needed to ensure compliance with fundamental rights. Beyond this, the AI system's capabilities and limitations should be communicated to AI practitioners or end-users in a manner appropriate to the use case at hand. This could encompass communication of the AI system's level of accuracy, as well as its limitations.

1.5 Diversity, non-discrimination and fairness

In order to achieve Trustworthy AI, we must enable inclusion and diversity throughout the entire AI system's life cycle. Besides the consideration and involvement of all affected stakeholders throughout the process, this also entails ensuring equal access through inclusive design processes as well as equal treatment. This requirement is closely linked with *the principle of fairness*.

Avoidance of unfair bias. Data sets used by AI systems (both for training and operation) may suffer from the inclusion of inadvertent historic bias, incompleteness and bad governance models. The continuation of such biases could lead to unintended (in)direct prejudice and discrimination against certain groups or people, potentially exacerbating prejudice and marginalisation. Harm can also result from the intentional exploitation of (consumer) biases or by engaging in unfair competition, such as the homogenisation of prices by means of collusion or a non-transparent market. Identifiable and discriminatory bias should be removed in the collection phase where possible. The way in which AI systems are developed (e.g. algorithms' programming) may also suffer from unfair bias. This could be counteracted by putting in place oversight processes to analyse and address the system's purpose, constraints, requirements and decisions in a clear and transparent manner. Moreover, hiring from diverse backgrounds, cultures and disciplines can ensure diversity of opinions and should be encouraged.

Accessibility and universal design. Particularly in business-to-consumer domains, systems should be user-centric and designed in a way that allows all people to use AI products or services, regardless of their age, gender, abilities or characteristics. Accessibility to this technology for persons with disabilities, which are present in all societalgroups, is of particular importance. AI systems should not have a one-size-fits-all approach and should consider Universal Design principles addressing the widest possible range of users, following relevant accessibility standards. This will enable equitable access and active participation of all people in existing and emerging computer-mediated human activities and with regard to assistive technologies.

Stakeholder Participation. In order to develop AI systems that are trustworthy, it is advisable to consult stakeholders who may directly or indirectly be affected by the system throughout its life cycle. It is beneficial to solicit regular feedback even after deployment and set up longer term mechanisms for stakeholder participation, for example by ensuring workers information, consultation and participation throughout the whole process of implementing AI systems at organisations.

1.6 Societal and environmental well-being

In line with the *principles of fairness* and *prevention of harm*, the broader society, other sentient beings and the environment should be also considered as stakeholders throughout the AI system's life cycle. Sustainability and ecological responsibility of AI systems should be encouraged, and research should be fostered into AI solutions addressing areas of global concern, such as for instance the Sustainable Development Goals. Ideally, AI systems should be used to benefit all human beings, including future generations.

Sustainable and environmentally friendly AI. AI systems promise to help tackling some of the most pressing societal concerns, yet it must be ensured that this occurs in the most environmentally friendly way possible. The system's development, deployment and use process, as well as its entire supply chain, should be assessed in this regard, e.g. via a critical examination of the resource usage and energy consumption during training, opting for less harmful choices. Measures securing the environmental friendliness of AI systems' entire supply chain should be encouraged.

Social impact. Ubiquitous exposure to social AI systems in all areas of our lives (be it in education, work, care or entertainment) may alter our conception of social agency, or impact our social relationships and attachment. While AI systems can be used to enhance social skills, they can equally contribute to their deterioration. This could also affect people's physical and mental wellbeing. The effects of these systems must therefore be carefully monitored and considered.

Society and Democracy. Beyond assessing the impact of an AI system's development, deployment and use on individuals, this impact should also be assessed from a societal perspective, taking into account its effect on institutions, democracy and society at large. The use of AI systems should be given careful consideration particularly in situations relating to the democratic process, including not only political decision-making but also electoral contexts.

1.7 Accountability

The requirement of accountability complements the above requirements, and is closely linked to the *principle of fairness*. It necessitates that mechanisms be put in place to ensure responsibility and accountability for AI systems and their outcomes, both before and after their development, deployment and use.

Auditability. Auditability entails the enablement of the assessment of algorithms, data and design processes. This does not necessarily imply that information about business models and intellectual property related to the AI system must always be openly available. Evaluation by internal and external auditors, and the availability of such evaluation reports, can contribute to the trustworthiness of the technology. In applications affecting fundamental rights, including safety-critical applications, AI systems should be able to be independently audited.

Minimisation and reporting of negative impacts. Both the ability to report on actions or decisions that contribute to a certain system outcome, and to respond to the consequences of such an outcome, must be ensured. Identifying, assessing, documenting and minimising the potential negative impacts of AI systems is especially crucial for those (in)directly affected. Due protection must be available for whistle-blowers, NGOs, trade unions or other entities when reporting legitimate concerns about an AI system. The use of impact assessments (e.g. red teaming or forms of Algorithmic Impact Assessment) both prior to and during the development, deployment and use of AI systems can be helpful to minimise negative impact. These assessments must be proportionate to the risk that the AI systems pose.

Trade-offs. When implementing the above requirements, tensions may arise between them, which may lead to inevitable trade-offs. Such trade-offs should be addressed in a rational and methodological manner within the state of the art. This entails that relevant interests and values implicated by the AI system should be identified and that, if conflict arises, trade-offs should be explicitly acknowledged and evaluated in terms of their risk to ethical principles, including fundamental rights. In situations in which no ethically acceptable trade-offs can be identified, the development, deployment and use of the AI system should not proceed in that form. Any decision about which trade-off to make should be reasoned and properly documented. The decision-maker must be accountable for the manner in which the appropriate trade-off is being made, and should continually review the appropriateness of the resulting decision to ensure that necessary changes can be made to the system where needed.

Redress. When unjust adverse impact occurs, accessible mechanisms should be foreseen that ensure adequate redress. Knowing that redress is possible when things go wrong is key to ensure trust. Particular attention should be paid to vulnerable persons or groups.

2. Technical and non-technical methods to realise Trustworthy AI

To implement the above requirements, both technical and non-technical methods can be employed. These encompass all stages of an AI system's life cycle. An evaluation of the methods employed to implement the requirements, as well as reporting and justifying changes to the implementation processes, should occur on an ongoing basis. AI systems are continuously evolving and acting in a dynamic environment. ...

...

The following methods can be either complementary or alternative to each other, since different requirements – and different sensitivities – may raise the need for different methods of implementation. This overview is neither meant to be comprehensive or exhaustive, nor mandatory. Rather, its aim is to offer a list of suggested methods that may help to implement Trustworthy AI.

2.1. Technical methods

This section describes technical methods to ensure Trustworthy AI that can be incorporated in the design, development and use phases of an AI system. The methods listed below vary in level of maturity.

■ *Architectures for Trustworthy AI*

Requirements for Trustworthy AI should be "translated" into procedures and/or constraints on procedures, which should be anchored in the AI system's architecture. This could be accomplished through a set of "white list" rules (behaviours or states) that the system should always follow, "black list" restrictions on behaviours or states that the system should never transgress, and mixtures of those or more complex provable guarantees regarding the system's behaviour. Monitoring of the system's compliance with these restrictions during operations may be achieved by a separate process.

AI systems with learning capabilities that can dynamically adapt their behaviour can be understood as non-deterministic systems possibly exhibiting unexpected behaviour. These are often considered through the theoretical lens of a "sense-plan-act" cycle. Adapting this architecture to ensure Trustworthy AI requires the requirements' integration at all three steps of the cycle: (i) at the "sense"-step, the system should be developed such that it recognises all environmental elements necessary to ensure adherence to the requirements; (ii) at the "plan"-step, the system should only consider plans that adhere to the requirements; (iii) at the "act"-step, the system's actions should be restricted to behaviours that realise the requirements.

The architecture as sketched above is generic and only provides an imperfect description for most AI systems. Nevertheless, it gives anchor points for constraints and policies that should be reflected in specific modules to result in an overall system that is trustworthy and perceived as such.

■ *Ethics and rule of law by design (X-by-design)*

Methods to ensure values-by-design provide precise and explicit links between the abstract principles which the system is required to respect and the specific implementation decisions. The idea that compliance with norms can be implemented into the design of the AI system is key to this method. Companies are responsible for identifying the impact of their AI systems from the very start, as well as the norms their AI system ought to comply with to avert negative impacts. Different "by-design" concepts are already widely used, e.g. *privacy-by-design* and *security-by-design*. As indicated above, to earn trust AI needs to be secure in its processes, data and outcomes, and should be designed to be robust to adversarial data and attacks. It should implement a mechanism for fail-safe shutdown and enable resumed operation after a forced shut-down (such as an attack).

■ *Explanation methods*

For a system to be trustworthy, we must be able to understand why it behaved a certain way and why it provided a given interpretation. A whole field of research, Explainable AI (XAI) tries to address this issue to better understand the system's underlying mechanisms and find solutions. Today, this is still an open challenge for AI systems based on neural networks. Training processes with neural nets can result in network parameters set to numerical values that are difficult to correlate with results. Moreover, sometimes small changes in data values might result in dramatic changes in interpretation, leading the system to e.g. confuse a school bus with an ostrich. This vulnerability can also be exploited during attacks on the system. Methods involving XAI research are vital not only to explain the system's behaviour to users, but also to deploy reliable technology.

■ *Testing and validating*

Due to the non-deterministic and context-specific nature of AI systems, traditional testing is not enough. Failures of the concepts and representations used by the system may only manifest when a programme is applied to sufficiently realistic data. Consequently, to verify and validate processing of data, the underlying model must be carefully monitored during both training and deployment for its stability, robustness and operation within well-understood and predictable bounds. It must be ensured that the outcome of the planning process is consistent with the input, and that the decisions are made in a way allowing validation of the underlying process.

Testing and validation of the system should occur as early as possible, ensuring that the system behaves as intended throughout its entire life cycle and especially after deployment. It should include all components of an AI system, including data, pre-trained models, environments and the behaviour of the system as a whole. The testing processes should be designed and performed by an as diverse group of people as possible. Multiple metrics should be developed to cover the categories that are being tested for different perspectives. Adversarial testing by trusted and diverse "red teams" deliberately attempting to "break" the system to find vulnerabilities, and "bug bounties" that incentivise outsiders to detect and responsibly report system errors and weaknesses, can be considered. Finally, it must be ensured that the outputs or actions are consistent with the results of the preceding processes, comparing them to the previously defined policies to ensure that they are not violated.

■ *Quality of Service Indicators*

Appropriate quality of service indicators can be defined for AI systems to ensure that there is a baseline understanding as to whether they have been tested and developed with security and safety considerations in mind. These indicators could include measures to evaluate the testing and training of algorithms as well as traditional software metrics of functionality, performance, usability, reliability, security and maintainability.

2.2. Non-technical methods

This section describes a variety of non-technical methods that can serve a valuable role in securing and maintaining Trustworthy AI. These too should be evaluated on an **ongoing basis**.

■ *Regulation*

As mentioned above, regulation to support AI's trustworthiness already exists today – think of product safety legislation and liability frameworks. To the extent we consider that regulation may need to be revised, adapted or introduced, both as a safeguard and as an enabler, this will be raised in our second deliverable, consisting of AI Policy and Investment Recommendations.

■ *Codes of conduct*

Organisations and stakeholders can sign up to the Guidelines and adapt their charter of corporate responsibility, Key Performance Indicators ("KPIs"), their codes of conduct or internal policy documents to add the striving towards Trustworthy AI. An organisation working on or with AI systems can, more generally, document its intentions, as well as underwrite them with standards of certain desirable values such as fundamental rights, transparency and the avoidance of harm.

■ *Standardisation*

Standards, for example for design, manufacturing and business practices, can function as a quality management system for AI users, consumers, organisations, research institutions and governments by offering the ability to recognise and encourage ethical conduct through their purchasing decisions. Beyond conventional standards, co-regulatory approaches exist: accreditation systems, professional codes of ethics or standards for fundamental rights compliant design. Current examples are e.g. ISO Standards or the IEEE P7000 standards series, but in the future a possible 'Trustworthy AI' label might be suitable, confirming by reference to specific technical standards that the system, for instance, adheres to safety, technical robustness and transparency.

■ *Certification*

As it cannot be expected that everyone is able to fully understand the workings and effects of AI systems, consideration can be given to organisations that can attest to the broader public that an AI system is transparent, accountable and fair. These certifications would apply standards developed for different application domains and AI techniques, appropriately aligned with the industrial and societal standards of different contexts. Certification can however never replace responsibility. It should hence be complemented by accountability frameworks, including disclaimers as well as review and redress mechanisms.

■ *Accountability via governance frameworks*

Organisations should set up governance frameworks, both internal and external, ensuring accountability for the ethical dimensions of decisions associated with the development, deployment and use of AI systems. This can, for instance, include the appointment of a person in charge of ethics issues relating to AI systems, or an internal/external ethics panel or board. Amongst the possible roles of such a person, panel or board, is to provide oversight and advice. As set out above, certification specifications and bodies can also play a role to this end. Communication channels should be ensured with industry and/or public oversight groups, sharing best practices, discussing dilemmas or reporting emerging issues of ethical concerns. Such mechanisms can complement but cannot replace legal oversight (e.g. in the form of the appointment of a data protection officer or equivalent measures, legally required under data protection law).

■ *Education and awareness to foster an ethical mind-set*

Trustworthy AI encourages the informed participation of all stakeholders. Communication, education and training play an important role, both to ensure that knowledge of the potential impact of AI systems is widespread, and to make people aware that they can participate in shaping the societal development. This includes all stakeholders, e.g. those involved in making the products (the designers and developers), the users (companies or individuals) and other impacted groups (those who may not purchase or use an AI system but for whom decisions are made by an AI system, and society at large). Basic AI literacy should be fostered across society. A prerequisite for educating the public is to ensure the proper skills and training of ethicists in this space.

■ *Stakeholder participation and social dialogue*

The benefits of AI systems are many, and Europe needs to ensure that they are available to all. This requires an open discussion and the involvement of social partners and stakeholders, including the general public. Many organisations already rely on stakeholder panels to discuss the use of AI systems and data analytics. These panels include various members, such as legal experts, technical experts, ethicists, consumer representatives and workers. Actively seeking participation and dialogue on the use and impact of AI systems supports the evaluation of results and approaches, and can particularly be helpful in complex cases.

■ *Diversity and inclusive design teams*

Diversity and inclusion play an essential role when developing AI systems that will be employed in the real world. It is critical that, as AI systems perform more tasks on their own, the teams that design, develop, test and maintain, deploy and procure these systems reflect the diversity of users and of society in general. This contributes to objectivity and consideration of different perspectives, needs and objectives. Ideally, teams are not only diverse in terms of gender, culture, age, but also in terms of professional backgrounds and skill sets.

...

Chapter III: Assessing Trustworthy AI

Based on the key requirements of Chapter II, this Chapter sets out a non-exhaustive **Trustworthy AI assessment list** (pilot version) to **operationalise Trustworthy AI**. It particularly applies to AI systems that directly interact with users, and is primarily addressed to developers and deployers of AI systems (whether self-developed or acquired from third parties). This assessment list does not address the operationalisation of the first component of Trustworthy AI (lawful AI). Compliance with this assessment list is not evidence of legal compliance, nor is it intended as guidance to ensure compliance with applicable law. Given the application-specificity of AI systems, the assessment list will need to be tailored to the specific use case and context in which the system operates. In addition, this chapter offers a general recommendation on how to implement the assessment list for Trustworthy AI through a governance structure embracing both operational and management level.

The assessment list and governance structure will be developed in close collaboration with stakeholders across the public and private sector. The process will be driven as a piloting process, allowing for extensive feedback from two parallel processes:

> a) a qualitative process, ensuring representability, where a small selection of companies, organisations and institutions (from different sectors and of different sizes) will sign up to pilot the assessment list and the governance structure in practice and to provide in-depth feedback;

> b) a quantitative process where all interested stakeholders can sign up to pilot the assessment list and provide feedback through an open consultation.

After the piloting phase, we will integrate the results from the feedback process into the assessment list and prepare a revised version in early 2020. The aim is to achieve a framework that can be horizontally used across all applications and hence offer a foundation for ensuring Trustworthy AI in all domains. Once such foundation has been established, a sectorial or application-specific framework could be developed.

■ *Governance*

Stakeholders may wish to consider how the Trustworthy AI assessment list can be implemented in their organisation. This can be done by incorporating the assessment process into existing governance mechanisms, or by implementing new processes. This choice will depend on the internal structure of the organisation as well as its size and available resources.

> …

■ *Using the Trustworthy AI assessment list[1]*

---

[1] Available at: https://ec.europa.eu/futurium/en/ai-alliance-consultation/guidelines#Top [footnote not in original]

When using the assessment list in practice, we recommend paying attention not only to the areas of concern but also to the questions that cannot be (easily) answered. One potential problem might be the lack of diversity of skills and competences in the team developing and testing the AI system, and therefore it might be necessary to involve other stakeholders inside or outside the organisation. It is strongly recommended to log all results both in technical terms and in management terms, ensuring that the problem solving can be understood at all levels in the governance structure.

This assessment list is meant to guide AI practitioners to achieve Trustworthy AI. The assessment should be tailored to the specific use case in a proportionate way. During the piloting phase, specific sensitive areas might be revealed and the need for further specifications in such cases will be evaluated in the next steps. While this assessment list does not provide concrete answers to address the raised questions, it encourages reflection on how Trustworthy AI can be operationalised, and on the potential steps that should be taken in this regard.

■ *Relation to existing law and processes*

It is also important for AI practitioners to recognise that there are various existing laws mandating particular processes or prohibiting particular outcomes, which may overlap and coincide with some of the measures listed in the assessment list. For example, data protection law sets out a series of legal requirements that must be met by those engaged in the collection and processing of personal data. Yet, because Trustworthy AI also requires the ethical handling of data, internal procedures and policies aimed at securing compliance with data protection laws might also help to facilitate ethical data handling and can hence complement existing legal processes. Compliance with this assessment list is *not*, however, evidence of legal compliance, nor is it intended as guidance to ensure compliance with applicable laws.

Moreover, many AI practitioners already have existing assessment tools and software development processes in place to ensure compliance also with non-legal standards. The below assessment should not necessarily be carried out as a stand-alone exercise, but can be incorporated into such existing practices.

Council of Europe, Draft Recommendation of the Committee of Ministers to Member States on Human Rights Impacts of Algorithmic Systems (2019)

Preamble

1. Member States of the Council of Europe have committed themselves to ensuring the rights and freedoms enshrined in the Convention for the Protection of Human Rights and Fundamental Freedoms (ETS No. 5, "the Convention") to everyone within their jurisdiction. This commitment stands throughout the continuous processes of technological advancement and digital transformation that European societies are experiencing. As a result, member States must ensure that the design, development and implementation of algorithmic systems occur in compliance with human rights, with a view to harvesting positive effects and preventing or minimising possible adverse effects.

2. Human rights and fundamental freedoms are universal, indivisible, inter-dependent and interrelated. The use of digital applications as essential tools of everyday life, including in communication, education, health, agriculture and transportation, is rising in an unprecedented manner. They also play an increasing role in governance structures and the management and distribution of resources. Therefore, the application of algorithmic systems that have automated data collection, analytics, decision, or machine learning capacities has an evolving impact, which may be positive or negative, on the exercise, enjoyment and protection of all human rights and fundamental freedoms.

3. For the purposes of this recommendation, algorithmic systems are understood as applications that, often using various optimisation techniques, perform one or more tasks such as gathering, combining, cleaning, sorting and classifying data, as well as selection, prioritisation, recommendation and decision- making. Relying on one or more algorithms to fulfill their requirements in the settings in which they are applied, algorithmic systems increasingly permeate many aspects of contemporary human life.

4. Operating principally by detecting patterns in large datasets, algorithmic systems offer the potential to improve the performance of services (particularly through increased precision and targeting), provide new solutions, and deliver enormous efficiency and effectiveness gains in task and system performance. They have led to immense improvements in the categorisation and searchability of digital information and have facilitated important advances in fields such as

medical diagnostics, transportation and logistics, enabling the broader and faster sharing of information globally and allowing novel forms of coordination. Algorithmic systems can strengthen individual autonomy and self-determination and can enhance the exercise of human rights, for instance, by broadening access to information or by facilitating the enjoyment of the freedom of assembly and association, including by creating innovative ways of associating with others.

5. However, there are also significant human rights challenges attached to the increasing reliance on algorithmic systems in everyday life. Their functionality is frequently based on the systematic aggregation and analysis of data collected through the digital tracking of online and offline behaviour of individuals and groups at scale. In addition to personal data protection and privacy costs, tracking at scale can have an important chilling effect on the freedom of expression and other human rights. While it is often argued that these concerns are justified by gains in rationalisation and accuracy, it is important to note that algorithmic systems are based on statistical models of which errors form an inevitable part, sometimes with feedback loops that replicate, reinforce and prolong pre-existing errors and assumptions. Although it may seem as if larger datasets provide better chances of finding recurrent patterns and correlations, accuracy rates do not automatically increase with the size of the dataset. As a result of the abundance of data used in automated processes, the number of errors in the form of false positives and false negatives, and of people who are affected by these errors and inbuilt bias, will also expand, triggering additional interferences with the exercise of human rights in multiple ways.

6. Data-driven algorithmic systems do not process and generate outputs only on the basis of personal information and data. Sometimes, they are also based on non-observational and non-personal data such as simulations, synthetic data, or generalised rules, norms, procedures or laws. However, human rights may still be negatively affected at the point of use of such algorithms, even if they are trained only on synthetic data. Individuals and groups whose data is not processed or who have not otherwise been taken into consideration may also be directly concerned and significantly impacted, particularly when algorithmic systems are used to inform decision-making, adjust recommendations, or shape physical environments.

7. Many algorithmic systems use optimisation techniques where development and implementation stages are tightly entangled, as each use of the algorithmic system can be used to prompt adjustments in its functioning towards better achievement of results that are based on a narrow range of pre-defined outcomes. Such processes can shape and disrupt environments, particularly when operating at scale, as they prioritise certain values over others, for instance profit orientation over accessibility, in ways that are often not transparent, not accountable, not controllable by the affected individual, and neither serving his or her interest nor promoting collective welfare.

8. Given the wide range of types and applications of algorithmic systems in everyday life, the level of their impact – positive and negative – on human rights will always depend on the specific purpose for which they are used, their functionality and the scale at which they are deployed. It will also depend on the broader organisational, thematic, societal and legal context in which they are implemented, each associated with specific public and ethical values. Applications may be very diverse, such as for e-mail spam filters, for health-related data analytics, or for rationalising traffic flows. They may also be applied for predictive purposes in the context of policing and border control, for the purposes of combatting money laundering and fraud, or in labour, employment and educational settings, including as part of public and private recruitment and selection processes.

9. When assessing a potential negative human rights impact stemming from the design, development and implementation of an algorithmic system, it is therefore necessary to evaluate continuously and document in what context, for what purpose, with what accuracy, with what performance indicators and at what scale the system is used.

10. In many instances, the human rights impact will not attain the 'minimum level of severity' for any given individual that renders it significant in terms of corresponding state obligations or private actor responsibilities. Yet the same system may impact collectively upon particular groups or the population at large, triggering substantial and systematic impacts on human rights that member States should consider. For the purposes of this recommendation, the term "significant human rights impact" thus denotes relevant individual-level or systematic impacts on human rights, that engage state obligations vis-à-vis human rights.

11. In some cases, the application of an algorithmic system may prompt a particular, higher risk to human rights, for instance because it is used by states for their public service or public policy delivery and the individual does not have a possibility to opt out. A similarly heightened risk ensues as a result of use in the context of decision-making processes, by either public authorities or private parties, in situations that carry particular weight or legal consequences. For example, the automated classification and selection of applications for bank loans can lead to the social sorting of financially weak groups or to the disruption of housing and labour markets. In this recommendation, the term "high risk" is applied when referring to the use of algorithmic systems in processes or decisions that can produce serious consequences for individuals or in situations where the lack of alternatives prompts a particularly high probability of human rights infringement.

12. Deserving of particular attention in the assessment of potential negative human rights impacts — and resulting questions of responsibility allocation — is the wide range of uses of algorithmic systems that are neither clearly public nor clearly private. This may be the case when parts of a public service are outsourced to private sector providers, who may themselves depend on other service providers, when public entities procure algorithmic systems and servicing from the private sector, or when a company deploys an algorithmic system in order to achieve public policy objectives defined by States.

13. Complicated are also cases when functions traditionally performed by public authorities, such as related to transport or telecommunications, become reliant in full or in part on the provision of algorithmic systems by private parties. When such systems are then withdrawn for commercial reasons, the result can range from decrease in quality and/or efficiency to the loss of essential services by individuals and communities. States should have contingencies in place to ensure that essential services remain available irrespective of their commercial viability, particularly in circumstances where private sector actors dominate the market in ways that place them in positions of influence or even control.

14. The design, development, and implementation of algorithmic systems engages many actors, including software designers, programmers, data sources, data workers, proprietors, sellers, users or customers, providers of infrastructure, and public and private actors and institutions. In addition, many algorithmic systems, whether learning or non-learning, operate with significant levels of opacity. Even the designer or operator, who will usually establish the overarching aim and parameters of the system, including the input data, the optimisation target and the model, is likely to encounter uncertainty about the direct and indirect effects of the system on users and the broader environments in which these systems are intended to operate.

15. While digital technologies hold significant potential for economic growth and socially beneficial innovation, the achievement of these goals must be rooted in the shared values of democratic societies. Rule of law standards that govern public and private relations in the "analogue world", such as transparency, predictability, accountability and oversight, must also be maintained in the context of algorithmic systems. While on-going public and private sector initiatives intended to develop ethical guidelines and standards for the design, development and implementation of algorithmic systems represent highly welcome recognition of the risks that these systems pose for normative values, they do not relieve Council of Europe member States from their obligations as primary guardians of the Convention.

16. In order to live up to their obligations under the Convention, member States must refrain from direct or indirect violations through algorithmic systems, whether employed by themselves or as a result of their actions. It is essential that member States be aware of the specific human rights impacts of these processes, and that any investment in such systems contain adequate contingencies for meaningful assessment, review processes and redress for ensuing adverse effects or, where necessary, abandonment of processes that fail to meet minimum human rights standards.

17. In addition to the above commitments, the Convention also contains positive obligations for member States to establish effective and predictable legislative, regulatory and supervisory frameworks that prevent, detect, prohibit and remedy human rights violations, whether stemming from public or private actors, whether affecting relations between businesses, between businesses and consumers or between businesses and other affected individuals and groups. Member States should ensure compliance with applicable legislative and regulatory frameworks and guarantee procedural, organisational and substantive safeguards and access to effective remedies vis-à-vis all relevant actors. They should further promote an environment in which technological innovation respects and enhances human rights and complies with the fundamental obligation that all human rights restrictions be necessary, proportionate and implemented in accordance with the law.

18. Private sector actors, due to the horizontal effects of human rights and in line with the UN Guiding Principles on Business and Human Rights, have the corporate responsibility to respect the human rights of their customers and of all affected parties. To this end, flexible governance models should be adopted that guarantee fast reparation and redress when incidents occur, ensuring that responsibility and accountability for the protection of human rights are effectively and clearly distributed throughout all stages of the process, from task identification to data selection, collection and analysis, to system modelling and design, through to deployment and implementation, review and reporting requirements. Risk management processes should detect and prevent detrimental use of algorithmic systems, negative impacts or disproportionately high risks, and include the possibility of refusing deployment of certain systems when this is proportional to the possible direct or indirect harms for human rights.

19. Against this background, and in order to provide guidance to all relevant actors who are obliged to protect and respect human rights in the contemporary, global and technology-driven environment, the Committee of Ministers, under the terms of Article 15.b of the Statute of the Council of Europe (ETS No. 1), recommends that member States:

- fully implement the Guidelines set out in the Appendix of this Recommendation;

- in implementing the Guidelines, take account of their relevant obligations under the Convention, the European Social Charter (ETS No. 35 and ETS 163), the Convention for the Protection of Individuals with regard to Automatic Processing of Personal Data as modernised in the Amending Protocol (CETS No. 223, "modernised Convention 108"), the Convention on Cybercrime (ETS No. 185, "the Budapest Convention"), the Council of Europe Convention on the Protection of Children against Sexual Exploitation and Sexual Abuse (CETS No. 201, "the Lanzarote Convention") and the Council of Europe Convention on Preventing and Combating Violence against Women and Domestic Violence (CETS No. 210, "the Istanbul Convention");

- in implementing the Guidelines, take account of the relevant case law of the European Court of Human Rights and previous Committee of Ministers' recommendations and declarations, notably:

- fully comply with their positive obligation to ensure, when devising and implementing legislative, regulatory and supervisory frameworks related to algorithmic systems, that private sector actors engaged in the design, development and implementation of algorithmic systems, fulfil their responsibilities to respect human rights in particular with regard to the United Nations Guiding Principles on Business and Human Rights;

- promote the goals of this Recommendation at the national level and all relevant international and regional forums; engage in, and ensure the representativeness and balance of, a regular, inclusive, meaningful and transparent dialogue, paying particular attention to the needs and voices of vulnerable groups, with all relevant stakeholders, which may include civil society, the private sector, media, education establishments, academia, as well as infrastructure providers and basic public services, including welfare and policing, with a view to sharing and discussing information, coordinating initiatives, and monitoring and assessing the responsible use of algorithmic systems that impact the exercise and enjoyment of human rights and related legal and policy issues;

- prioritise the building of expertise in public and private institutions involved in integrating algorithmic systems into aspects of societies with a view to effectively protecting human rights;

- encourage and promote the implementation of effective and tailored media, digital and information literacy programmes to support all individuals and groups to enjoy the benefits and minimise the exposure to risks stemming from the use of algorithmic systems, in effective co-operation with all relevant stakeholders, including from the private sector, media, civil society, education establishments, academia and technical institutions;

- review regularly and report on the measures taken to implement this recommendation and its guidelines with a view to enhancing their effectiveness.

- Recommendation CM/Rec(2018)2 on the roles and responsibilities of internet intermediaries;

- CM/Rec(2016)3 of the Committee of Ministers to member States on human rights and business; Recommendation CM/Rec(2014)6 on a Guide to human rights for Internet users; Recommendation CM/Rec(2012)3 on the protection of human rights with regard to search engines;

- Recommendation CM/Rec(2012)4 on the protection of human rights with regard to social networking services;

- Recommendation CM/Rec(2010)13 on the protection of individuals with regard to automatic processing of personal data in the context of profiling,

- Recommendation CM/Rec(2007)16 on measures to promote the public service value of the Internet;

- Committee of Ministers Declaration CM/Decl(13/02/2019)1 on the manipulative capabilities of algorithmic processes;

- the Guidelines on Artificial Intelligence and Data Protection T-PD(2019)01;

- the 2017 Guidelines on the protection of individuals with regard to the processing of personal data in a world of Big Data,

- the 2016 Venice Commission Rule of Law checklist CDL-AD(2016)007 and related international standards.

Appendix to Recommendation CM(20xx)x

Guidelines for States regarding the human rights impacts of algorithmic systems

These guidelines are designed to advise states and private sector actors in all their actions regarding the design, development and implementation of algorithmic systems. To ensure that the human rights and fundamental freedoms of all individuals and affected parties, as enshrined in the Convention and other relevant treaties, be effectively protected throughout technological evolution, member States of the Council of Europe shall refrain from violating human rights through the use of algorithmic systems, and shall establish legislative and regulatory frameworks that foster an environment where all actors respect and promote human rights and seek to prevent possible infringements. Independently of that and across jurisdictions, private sector actors have the responsibility to respect internationally recognised human rights.

A – Obligation of states with respect to the protection and promotion of human rights and fundamental freedoms in the context of algorithmic systems

1 General principles

1.1 Enacting legislation: The process of drafting and enacting legislation or regulation applicable to the design, development and implementation of algorithmic systems should be transparent, accountable and inclusive. States should regularly consult with all relevant stakeholders and affected parties.

1.2 **Computational experimentation**: States should ensure that any form of computational experimentation, such as AB testing processes, be conducted only after a meaningful human rights impact assessment. The free, specific, informed and unambiguous consent of participating individuals should be sought in advance. Experimentation designed to produce deceptive or exploitative effects should be explicitly prohibited. An accessible means of withdrawing consent is also essential. Immature software applications should not be tested on individuals, groups, or populations.

1.3 **Empowerment**: States should consider media, digital and information literacy that enables the competent and critical use of digital technologies as an essential skill for all involved in and affected by the design, development and implementation of algorithmic systems. All relevant actors, including private sector actors, media, education establishments, academia and technical institutions, should promote, in a tailored and inclusive manner (taking account of diversity with respect to, for instance, age, gender, race, ethnicity or socio-economic background), appropriate levels of understanding of the functioning of algorithmic systems and of the human rights risks stemming from their use in everyday life, enhancing the ability of all users to be aware of their rights and freedoms and use these technologies for their benefit.

1.4 **Institutional frameworks**: States should identify appropriate institutional and regulatory frameworks and standards that set benchmarks and safeguards to ensure the human rights compatibility of the design, development and implementation of algorithmic systems. Efforts should ensure that direct or indirect human rights risks, including possible cumulative effects of discrete systems, can be promptly identified and adequate remedial action initiated. States should invest in relevant technical, legal and ethical expertise to be available in adequately resourced regulatory and supervisory authorities. They should further closely co-operate with universities, standard-setting organisations, operators of services, developers of algorithmic systems and relevant non-governmental organisations of diverse backgrounds.

2 Data management

2.1 **Interoperability**: States should ensure that all design, development, and implementation of algorithmic systems provide an avenue for individuals to analyse, manage, export and transfer their data, including through the use of interoperable data and output formats. Deliberate efforts by individuals or groups to make themselves, their physical environment or their activities illegible to automation or other forms of machine reading should be recognised as valid exercise of informational self-determination, subject to possible restrictions provided for by law.

2.2 Datasets: In the design, development, implementation and procurement of algorithmic systems for or by them, States should carefully assess what human rights may be affected as a result of the types of data that are being inputted or outputted into and from an algorithmic system, as these may stand in as a proxy for classifiers such as gender, race, religion, or social origin. The shortcomings of the dataset, the possibility of its inappropriate use, the negative externalities resulting from these shortcomings and inappropriate uses as well as the environments within which the dataset will be or could possibly be used, should also be assessed carefully. Particular attention should be paid to inherent risks, such as the possible re-identification of individuals using data that was previously processed on the basis of anonymity or pseudonymity, and the generation of new, inferred, potentially sensitive personal data and forms of categorisation through automated means. Based on these assessments, States should take appropriate action to prevent, where possible, or otherwise effectively minimise adverse effects.

2.3 Infrastructure: States should invest in and develop infrastructures for data processing and storage that is safe and secure, with a view to achieving effective capacity to respond to the increasing centralisation of data and data processing capacity (including in cloud processing) in the hands of a few companies and ensuring that high quality data processing and computational capabilities remain accessible to public and private actors alike.

3 Analysis and modelling

3.1 Embedding of safeguards: States should ensure that, whenever appropriate, algorithmic design, development, and implementation processes embed safety, privacy, data protection, and security safeguards by design, with a view to preventing and minimising human rights violations and other adverse effects on individuals and society. Certification schemes based on international standards should be designed and applied for labelling provenance and quality assessment of datasets. Such safeguards should also form part of procurement processes and should be informed by and compliant with regulatory frameworks that ban certain uses of algorithmic systems.

3.2 Testing: Regular testing, evaluation, reporting and auditing against state of the art standards related to completeness, relevance, privacy, data protection and security infringements before, during and after production and deployment should form integral part of these efforts, in particular where automated systems produce real-time effects. Efforts should include an evaluation of the legality, desirability and legitimacy of the goal that the system intends to achieve or optimise. Such evaluation should also form part of procurement processes. Any significant restrictions on human rights that are identified during testing of such systems should result in immediate rectification and, failing that, suspension of the system until such rectifications can take place.

3.3 Evaluation of datasets and system externalities: States should ensure that the functioning of algorithmic systems that they implement is tested and evaluated with due regard to the fact that outputs vary according to the specific context of the deployment and the size and nature of the dataset that was used to train the system, in particular with regard to bias and discriminatory outputs. Depending on the potential impact of the algorithmic system on human rights and in order to avoid compromising other human rights, testing should, where possible, be performed without using real personal data of individuals, and should be informed through a diverse and representative stakeholder process, taking due account of the externalities of the proposed system on populations and their environments before and after deployment. States should further be aware of the possibility and risks of testing samples or outputs being reused in contexts other than those for which the system was originally developed for, including when used for the development of other algorithmic systems. This should not be permitted without new testing and evaluation of the appropriateness of such uses.

3.4 Testing on personal data: States should ensure that the evaluation and testing of algorithmic systems on personal data of individuals be performed with diverse, sufficiently representative sample populations. Relevant demographic groups should be neither over - nor under - represented. States should also ensure that staff involved in such activities is from sufficiently diverse backgrounds to avoid deliberate or accidental bias. Furthermore, they should ensure that the development of algorithmic systems be discontinued if testing or deployment involves the externalisation of risks or costs on to particular individuals, groups, populations and their environments. Relevant legislative frameworks should disincentivise such externalisation of risks or costs.

3.5 Parallel modelling: As regards the use of algorithmic systems in the delivery of public services and in other high risk contexts in which States use such technologies, alternative and parallel modelling should be performed using other methods in order to ensure that the performance and output of the algorithmic model can be adequately tested in comparison to other options.

4 Transparency, contestability and effective remedies

4.1 Levels of transparency: States should establish minimum levels of transparency about the use, design and basic processing criteria and methods of algorithmic systems implemented by and for them or by private sector actors. The legislative frameworks for intellectual property or trade secrets should not preclude such transparency, nor should states or private parties seek to exploit them for this purpose.

4.2 Identifiability of algorithmic decision-making: States should ensure that all selection processes or decisions taken or aided by algorithmic systems that may significantly impact the exercise of human rights, whether in the public or private sphere, be identifiable as such and provide the necessary information to allow for meaningful human review and contestation, in both process and rationale. The use of algorithmic systems in decision-making processes that carry high risks to human rights should be accompanied by particularly high standards of explainability of processes and outputs.

4.3 Meaningful contestability: States should ensure that appropriate regulatory frameworks exist to guarantee a meaningful right to contest relevant determinations and decisions. As a necessary precondition, the existence, operation, reasoning and possible outcome of algorithmic systems at individual and collective level should be explained and clarified in a timely, impartial, user-friendly and accessible manner to individuals whose rights may be affected, as well as to relevant public authorities. The right to contest may not be waived, and should be affordable and easily enforceable before, during and after deployment, including through the provision of easily accessible contact points and hotlines.

4.4 Adequate oversight: States should ensure that adequate oversight is maintained over the number and type of contestations made by affected individuals or groups against certain algorithmic systems that are directly or indirectly implemented by or for them, with a view to ensuring that the results do not only lead to remedial action in the specific case but are also fed into the systems themselves so as to avoid repetitions, seek improvement, and possibly discontinue the introduction or on-going deployment of certain systems due to their human rights risks. Information on these contestations and resulting follow- up action should be documented regularly and made publicly available.

4.5 Effective remedies: States should ensure accessible, affordable, independent and effective judicial and non-judicial procedures that guarantee the impartial review, in compliance with Articles 6 and 13 of the Convention, of all claims of direct and indirect violations of Convention rights through the use of algorithmic systems, whether stemming from public or private sector actors. Through their legislative frameworks, they should ensure that individuals and groups are afforded with access to prompt, transparent, functional and effective remedies with respect to their grievances, including apology, deletion or rectification of data, annulment of the automated decision or compensation for damages. Judicial review should remain available and accessible, when internal and alternative dispute settlement mechanisms prove insufficient or when either of the affected parties opts for judicial redress or appeal.

4.6 Barriers: States should proactively seek to reduce all legal, practical or other relevant barriers that could lead to directly or indirectly affected individuals and groups being denied an effective remedy to their grievances. This includes the necessity to ensure that adequately trained staff is available to review the case competently and take appropriate action effectively.

5 Precautionary measures

5.1 Indicators: States should cooperate with each other and with private sector actors and relevant rights groups to develop and implement appropriate indicators, criteria and methods for state of the art human rights impact assessment processes to be conducted with regard to all algorithmic systems with potentially significant human rights impacts, with a view to evaluating potential risks and tracking actual harms, especially when such mechanisms are applied for non-targeted, explorative purposes.

5.2 Human rights impact assessments: States should ensure that they, as well as any private actors engaged to work with them or on their behalf, regularly conduct such human rights impact assessments prior to public procurement, during development, at regular milestones, and throughout their context-specific use to identify risks of rights-adverse outcomes. For algorithmic systems with high risks to human rights, impact assessments should include an evaluation of the possible transformations that they may bring upon existing social, institutional or governance structures.

5.3 Expertise and oversight: States should ensure that human rights impact assessments conducted by of for them are publicly accessible, have adequate expert input, and are effectively followed up. This may be supported by conducting dynamic testing methods and pre-release trials and by ensuring that potentially affected individuals and groups as well as relevant field experts are consulted and included as actors with real decision-making power, where appropriate, in the design, testing, and review phases. States should ensure that human rights impacts assessments related to high-risk algorithmic systems, whether produced in the public or private sphere, be submitted for independent expert review and inspection, and tiered processes should be created for independent oversight, including by judicial authorities when necessary.

5.4 Staff training: States should ensure that all relevant staff involved in the procurement, development, implementation and review of algorithmic systems with potentially significant human rights impacts are adequately trained with respect to applicable human rights norms and are aware of their duty to ensure not only a thorough technical review but also human rights compliance. Hiring practices should aim for diverse workforces to enhance the ability to consider multiple perspectives in the review processes. Such approaches should be documented with a view to promoting them beyond the public sector. States should also work together to share experiences and develop best practices.

5.5 Interactivity of systems: States should carefully monitor settings where multiple algorithmic systems operate in the same environment, or a given system bundles multiple algorithmic systems in order to identify and mitigate negative externalities, where responsibility is difficult to apportion. States should utilise the mechanism of procurement or engagement of private services in public service delivery in full consideration of the need to maintain relevant oversight capacity, know-how, ownership and control over the use of algorithmic systems in multiple aspects of societies, with a view to avoiding path dependencies and preserving the viability of alternative solutions. Insofar as private sector actors provide services that are considered essential in modern society or have a de facto monopoly in providing such services, member States should develop regulatory frameworks that ensure effective enjoyment of human rights by affected individuals and groups. They should publicly account for their efforts in this regard.

5.6 Public debate: States should engage in inclusive, inter-disciplinary, informed and public debates to define what areas of public services affecting the exercise of human rights may not be determined, decided or optimised through algorithmic systems.

6 Empowerment through research, innovation and public awareness

6.1 Rights-promoting technology: States should promote the development of algorithmic systems and technologies that enhance equal access to and enjoyment of human rights and fundamental freedoms through the use of tax, procurement, or other incentives. This includes the development of mechanisms to evaluate the impact of algorithmic systems, the development of systems to address the needs of disadvantaged and underrepresented populations, as well as necessary efforts to ensure the sustainability of basic services through analogue means, both as contingency and as an effective opportunity for individuals to opt out.

6.2 Advancement of public benefit: States should engage in and support independent research aimed at assessing, testing and advancing the potential of algorithmic systems for creating positive human rights effects and for advancing public benefit. This may require the anticipation and possible discouragement of influences that may exclusively favour most commercially viable optimisation processes.

6.3 Human-centric and sustainable innovation: States should promote innovative design and technological development in line with existing human rights norms, in particular with respect to social rights and internationally recognised labour and employment standards, to enhance internationally agreed sustainable development goals, including as regards extraction and exploitation of environmental resources, and to address existing environmental challenges, such as through initiatives towards fair and human-centric innovation.

6.4 Independent research: States should encourage independent research into the development of effective accountability mechanisms and solutions to existing responsibility gaps related to opacity, inexplicability and related incontestability of algorithmic systems. Appropriate mechanisms should be put in place to guarantee the impartiality, global representation, and protection of researchers, journalists and academics engaged in such independent research.

6.5 Control over data: States should investigate strategies to prevent the monopolisation of control over data and data processing capacity with a view to ensuring the independence and vitality of the public and private sector, promoting the design and development of algorithmic systems in the public interest, and curbing concentration of market power.

B. Responsibilities of private sector actors with respect to human rights and fundamental freedoms in the context of algorithmic systems

1 General principles

1.1 Responsibility to respect: Private sector actors engaged in the design, development, sale, deployment, implementation and servicing of algorithmic systems, whether in the public or private sphere, have the responsibility to respect internationally recognised human rights and fundamental freedoms of their customers and of other parties who are affected by their activities. This responsibility exists independently of States' ability or willingness to fulfil their human rights obligations. As part of fulfilling this responsibility, private sector actors should take continuing, proactive and reactive steps to ensure that they do not cause or contribute to human rights abuses and that their innovation processes are human rights-friendly.

1.2 Scale of measures: The responsibility of private sector actors to respect human rights and to employ adequate measures applies regardless of their size, sector, operational context, ownership structure or nature. The scale and complexity of the means through which they meet their responsibilities may vary, however, taking into account their means and the severity of the potential impact on human rights by their services and systems. Where different sets of private sector actors co-operate and contribute to potential human rights interferences, efforts from all partners are required and should be proportional to their respective impact and abilities.

1.3 Additional key standards: Given that the design, development and implementation of algorithmic systems engages private sector actors at many levels and often in close cooperation with public actors, some of the provisions that are outlined in Chapter A as obligations of States also translate into corporate responsibilities for private sector actors. Irrespective of whether corresponding regulatory action has been taken by States and in addition to the below provisions, private sector actors should uphold the standards contained in provisions 1.2, 1.3, 2.1, 3.1, 3.2, 4.2, 5.2 and 6.3 of Chapter A.

1.4 Discrimination: Private sector actors should produce and provide their products and services without discrimination. They should seek to ensure that the design, development or implementation of their algorithmic systems do not have direct or indirect discriminatory effects or harmful impacts on individuals or groups that are affected by these systems, including on those who have special needs or disabilities or may face structural inequalities in their access to human rights.

2 Data management

2.1 Consent rules: Private sector actors should ensure that individuals who are affected by their algorithmic systems with potential for significant human rights impacts are empowered with the choice to give and revoke free and informed consent regarding all use of their data, with both processes being equally easily accessible. Users should be further empowered to know how their data is being used, what the real and potential impact of the algorithmic system in question is, how to object to relevant processing of their data, and how to contest and challenge specific outputs. Consent rules for the use of tracking, storage and performance measurement tools of algorithmic systems must be clear, simply phrased, meaningful and complete.

2.2 Privacy settings: Private sector actors should facilitate the right of users to protect effectively their privacy while maintaining access to services, including through the possibility of choosing from a set of privacy setting options, presented in an easily visible, neutral and intelligible manner, or through the use of privacy enhancing technologies. Default options should lead only to the collection of data that are necessary for the specific purpose of the data processing. Any application of mechanisms to block, erase or quarantine user data, such as for security purposes, should be accompanied with due process guarantees and rapid remedies available in case of erroneous or disproportionate use.

3 Analysis and modelling

3.1 Data bias: Private sector actors should be cognisant of risks relating to quality, nature and origin of the data they are using for training their algorithmic systems, with a view to ensuring that bias and potential discrimination in datasets is adequately responded to within the specific context.

3.2 Sample populations: The evaluation and testing of algorithmic systems on personal data of individuals should be performed with diverse, sufficiently representative sample populations and not draw on or discriminate against any particular demographic group. Development of algorithmic systems should be discontinued or adjusted if development, testing or deployment involves the externalisation of risks or costs on to particular individuals, groups, populations and their environments.

3.3 Illegal access: Private sector actors should configure their algorithmic systems in such a way that it prevents illegal access, system interference and misuse of devices by third parties in line with applicable standards.

4 Transparency, contestability and effective remedies

4.1 Terms of service: Private sector actors should ensure that the use of algorithmic systems in the products and services they offer is made known to all affected parties, whether individual or legal entities, as well as to the general public in clear and plain language and in accessible formats. Terms of service should be easily understandable, containing clear and succinct language about possibilities for users to influence settings, about available options to change the features of the system, about applicable complaint mechanisms, the various stages of the procedure, the exact competencies of the contact points, indicative time frames and expected outcomes. All affected parties, new customers or customers of products and services whose application rules have been amended should be notified of relevant changes in a user-friendly format, and requested to consent to the changes where relevant. Failure to consent should not lead to essential services becoming unavailable.

4.2 Contestability: Private sector actors should make public information about the number and type of contests made by affected individuals or groups regarding the products and services they offer, with a view to ensuring that the results do not only lead to remedial action in the specific case but are also fed into the systems themselves to draw lessons from complaints and correct errors before harm occurs at massive scale.

4.3 Human review: In order to facilitate meaningful contestability, private sector actors should ensure that human reviewers remain accessible and that direct contact is made effectively possible, including through the provision of easily accessible contact points and hotlines. Individuals and groups should be allowed not only to contest but also to make suggestions for improvements and provide other useful feedback, including with respect to areas where human review is systematically required. All staff involved in the handling of customer complaints should be suitably versed in relevant human rights standards and benefit from regular training opportunities.

4.4 Effective remedies: Private sector actors should ensure that effective remedies and dispute resolution systems, including collective redress mechanisms, are available both online and offline to individuals, groups and legal entities, who wish to contest the introduction of a system with potential for human rights violations or remedy a violation of rights. The scope of available remedies may not be limited. All remedies should allow for an impartial and independent review, should be handled without unwarranted delays and should be conducted in good faith, with respect for due process guarantees. Relevant mechanisms should not negatively impact the opportunities for complainants to seek recourse through independent national, including judicial, review mechanisms. No waivers of rights or hindrances to the effective access to remedies may be included in their terms of service.

4.5 Participation: Private sector actors should actively engage in participatory processes with consumer associations, human rights advocates and other organisations representing the interests of individuals and affected parties, as well as with data protection and other independent administrative or regulatory authorities, for the design, implementation and evaluation of their complaint mechanisms, including collective redress mechanisms. Business associations should further invest – in cooperation with trade associations – in the establishment of model complaints mechanisms.

5 Precautionary measures

5.1 Continuous evaluation: Private sector actors should develop internal processes to ensure that their design, development and implementation of algorithmic systems is continuously evaluated and tested not only against possible technical errors but also against the potential legal, social and ethical impacts that the systems may carry. Where the application of algorithmic systems carries high risks to human rights, including through processes of micro-targeting, private sector actors should notify and consult supervisory authorities in all relevant jurisdictions to seek advice and guidance on how to manage these risks, including through the redesign of the services that led to the problematic outcome. Private sector actors should submit these algorithmic systems for regular independent expert review, and create tiered processes for independent oversight, including by judicial authorities when necessary.

5.2 Staff training: All relevant staff involved in human rights impact assessments and in the review of algorithmic systems should be adequately trained and aware of their responsibilities with respect to human rights including, but not limited to, applicable personal data protection and privacy standards.

5.3 Human rights impact assessments: Human rights impact assessments should be conducted as openly as possible and encourage active engagement of affected individuals and groups. In case of implementation of high-risk algorithmic systems, the results of human rights impacts assessment, identified techniques for risk mitigation, and relevant monitoring and review processes should be made publicly available, without prejudice to secrecy safeguarded by law. When secrecy rules need to be enforced, any confidential information should be provided in a separate annex to the assessment report. This annex shall not be public, but should be accessible by relevant supervisory authorities.

5.4 Follow up: Private sector actors should ensure appropriate follow-up to their human rights impact assessments by taking adequate action upon the findings and monitoring the effectiveness of identified responses, with a view to avoiding or mitigating adverse effects on and risks for the exercise of human rights. Identified failures should be resolved as quickly as possible and related activities suspended where appropriate. This requires regular and continued quality assurances checks and real-time auditing through design, testing, and deployment stages to monitor algorithmic systems for human rights impacts in context and in situ, and to correct errors and harms as appropriate. This is particularly important given the risk of feedback loops that can exacerbate and entrench negative outcomes.

6 Empowerment through research, innovation and public awareness

6.1 Research: Private sector actors should engage in ethical research aimed at assessing, testing and advancing the potential of algorithmic systems for creating positive human rights impacts and for advancing public benefit. They should also support independent research with this aim and respect the integrity of researchers and research institutions. This may include the development of mechanisms to evaluate the impact of algorithmic systems and the development of algorithmic systems to address the needs of disadvantaged and underrepresented populations.

6.2 Access to data: Private sector actors should provide access to relevant individual and meta-datasets in full respect of data protection legislation and principles, as well as access to data that has been classified for deletion, to independent researchers, journalists and academics engaged in analysing the impacts of algorithmic systems and digitalised services on the exercise of rights, on communication networks, and on democratic systems.

Japan, Draft AI R&D GUIDELINES
for International Discussions
(2019)

Table of Contents

Preface

Draft AI R&D GUIDELINES

[Attachment] Roles Expected to Be Taken by Related Stakeholders

...

Preface Research and development (R&D) and utilization of artificial intelligence (AI) are expected to progress dramatically in years to come. Under these circumstances, at the G7 Information and Communication Ministers Meeting in April 2016, Japan as the host nation introduced principles of AI development, over which the relevant ministers then held discussions. As a result, the G7 countries agreed that they will continue to lead the discussions of "AI R&D Principles" and "AI R&D Guidelines," which explains the principles, with the cooperation of international organizations such as OECD.

With proactive development and utilization of AI, Japan can solve various problems arising from challenges that it is confronted with (such as a declining birthrate and aging population). Moreover, with the findings obtained, Japan can make significant contributions to the international community by sharing matters that are expected to be taken into account in the AI development.

This draft is prepared as a basis for international discussions at G7 and OECD regarding matters expected to be considered in R&D activities for promoting the benefits and reducing the risks of AI. Considering that AI-related technologies are in the middle of development, it is NOT appropriate to treat international AI R&D Principles and AI R&D Guidelines, which explains the principles, as aimed for introduction of regulations. Rather, this draft is drawn up as a proposal of guidelines that will be internationally shared as non-regulatory and non-binding soft law. It is expected that the deliberations on such guidelines will:

• accelerate the participation of multistakeholders involved in R&D and utilization of AI (such as developers, service providers, users including civil society, governments, and international organizations) at both national and international levels, in the discussions towards establishing "AI R&D Guidelines" and "AI Utilization Guidelines"; and

• promote the international sharing of best practices in the R&D and utilization of AI, which will help gain the trust of users and the society in AI and facilitate the R&D and utilization of AI.

Draft AI R&D GUIDELINES[1]

1. Purpose

R&D and utilization of AI are expected to progress rapidly in years to come. In the process of the evolution of AI networking (that is a formation of networks in which AI systems are connected, over the Internet or other information-and-communication networks, to each other or to other types of systems (which is called "AI networks" hereafter)), enormous benefits are expected for humans as well as the society and the economy in such manners as making significant contributions to solving various problems that individuals, local communities, countries, and the international community[2]are confronted with. The R&D and utilization of AI should be accelerated in such a direction.

As part of this, from the viewpoint of promoting the benefits from AI systems to the society and the economy as well as mitigating the risks such as lack of transparency and loss of control, it becomes necessary to address relevant social, economic, ethical, and legal issues. In particular, services utilizing AI systems, like other information-and-communication ones, will be provided beyond national borders via networks; therefore, it is essential to share guidelines, which serve as non-regulatory and non-binding soft law, and their best practices among stakeholders (such as developers, service providers, users including civil society, governments, and international organizations) through open discussions to foster an international

---

[1] This draft has been prepared to be used for international discussions on the establishment of an internationally shared AI R&D Guidelines.

[2] For details on challenges faced by the international community, refer to the United Nations "Sustainable Development Goals" (SDGs) (http://www.un.org/ga/search/view_doc.asp?symbol=A/70/L.1)

consensus, so that the benefits from AI systems will be increased and risks with them be controlled.

In view of such awareness, the Guidelines aim at protecting the interests of users and deterring the spread of risks, thus achieving a human-centered "Wisdom Network Society"[3] by way of increasing the benefits and mitigating the risks of AI systems through the sound progress of AI networks.

To achieve the above-mentioned purpose, the Guidelines compile AI R&D Principles, which will be expected to be considered in AI-system development in the future, along with comments on the Guidelines.

While the R&D of AI systems covers various fields of the utilization, the benefits and risks of the AI systems might differ from field to field. The Guidelines set out matters common to those fields of AI utilization or matters expected to be considered with regard to the collaborations between the fields. On the other hand, for matters expected to be considered according to the circumstances of each field, it is hoped that discussions on guidelines for each field, including whether or not such guidelines should be established, will be held by concerned stakeholders including relevant international organizations in the fields, separately from the Guidelines.

Moreover, AI systems' outputs or programs might continuously change as a result of learning or other methods in the process of the utilization; therefore, while there are matters that the developers are expected to mind, there are other matters that users are expected to mind, too. For this reason, international discussions as to whether to formulate AI utilization guidelines are expected, in addition to the Guideline.

2. Basic Philosophies

Recognizing its purpose, the Guidelines shall be based upon five basic philosophies as follows:

1. To achieve **a human-centered society** where all human beings across the board enjoy the benefits from their life in harmony with AI networks, while human dignity and individual autonomy are respected.

---

[3] *A Wisdom Network Society* is a society where, as a result of the progress of AI networking, humans live in harmony with AI networks, and data/information/knowledge are freely and safely created, distributed, and linked to form a *wisdom network*, encouraging collaborations beyond space among people, things, and events in various fields and consequently enabling creative and vibrant developments.

2. To **share the Guidelines**, as non-binding soft law, **and their best practices internationally among stakeholders**, as, with the rapid development of the R&D and utilization of AI, networked AI systems are expected to have broad and significant impacts on human beings and society beyond national borders.

3. **To ensure an appropriate balance between the benefits and risks** of AI networks, so as to: (a) promote the benefits from AI networks through innovative and open R&D activities and fair competition; and (b) mitigate the risk that AI systems might infringe rights or interests, while fully respecting the value of the democratic society such as academic freedom and freedom of expression.

4. To make sure that AI R&D activities based on specific technologies or techniques are not hindered in light of **ensuring technological neutrality**, and **to be mindful that developers are not imposed of excessive burden**, as the rapid progress of AI-related technologies is anticipated to continue. And

5. **To constantly review the Guidelines and flexibly revise them as necessary** through international discussions, considering the extent of the progress of AI networking, because AI-related technologies and AI utilization are expected to continue to advance dramatically. Also, to strive for broad and flexible discussions including the involvement of related stakeholders, when reviewing the Guidelines.

3. Definition of Terms and Scope

3-1 Definition of Terms

In view of the basic philosophies stated in Section 2, the terms related to "AI" used in the Guidelines are defined as follows:

- "AI" refers to a concept that collectively refers to AI software and AI systems.[4]

---

[4] This definition of AI is assumed in the Guidelines to apply mainly to Narrow AI which has already been put into practical application. In anticipation of rapid technological progress related to AI such as autonomous AI and artificial general intelligence (AGI), however, it will also be able to cover various types of AI to be developed in the future if they have functions to change their own outputs or programs by learning or other methods.

  In the Guidelines, the definition of AI as described above, which comes from the standpoint of ensuring the technological neutrality set forth in the fourth basic philosophy, may apply to a variety of AI to be developed in the future depending on their functions. How to define AI in the Guidelines needs to be continuously discussed based on the trends of the technological progress of AI, etc.

• "AI software" refers to software that has functions to change its own outputs or programs in the process of the utilization, by learning data, information, or knowledge; or by other methods[5]. For example, machine learning software is classified into this category.

• "AI systems" refers to systems that incorporate AI software as a component. For instance, robots and cloud systems that implement AI software are classified into this category.

"Developers" and "users" of AI systems are defined as follows, although it should be noted that they are relative concepts in that who are developers or users depends on the situation:

• "Developers" refers to those who conduct the R&D of AI systems (which includes R&D using AI systems), including those providing to others AI-network services using AI systems that they have developed on their own.

• "Users" refers to those who use AI systems, including end users as well as providers who provide third parties with AI-network services developed by others.

3-2 Scope

The Guidelines cover **AI systems** that can be networked (i.e. connected to networks), since they can be used across national borders via networks, thereby widely bringing about benefits and risks to humans and society.

The Guidelines cover broadly all **developers** as defined in Section 3-1, given that the Guidelines serve as non-binding soft law.

The Guidelines cover **development** at a stage of connection to networks, but not include one within closed spaces (such as laboratories or sandboxes in which security is sufficiently ensured) in view of respect for academic freedom, the magnitude of the impact on society, and so on.

4. AI R&D Principles

(Principles mainly concerning the sound development of AI networking and the promotion of the benefits of AI systems)

---

[5] Methods other than learning, which might cause AI software to change its own outputs or programs, include inferences based on data, information, and knowledge; and interactions with the environment through sensors, actuators, etc.

1) **Principle of collaboration**—Developers should pay attention to the interconnectivity and interoperability of AI systems.

(Principles mainly concerning mitigation of risks associated with AI systems)

2) **Principle of transparency**—Developers should pay attention to the verifiability of inputs/outputs of AI systems and the explainability of their judgments.

3) **Principle of controllability**—Developers should pay attention to the controllability of AI systems.

4) **Principle of safety**—Developers should take it into consideration that AI systems will not harm the life, body, or property of users or third parties through actuators or other devices.

5) **Principle of security**—Developers should pay attention to the security of AI systems.

6) **Principle of privacy**—Developers should take it into consideration that AI systems will not infringe the privacy of users or third parties.

7) **Principle of ethics**—Developers should respect human dignity and individual autonomy in R&D of AI systems.

(Principles mainly concerning improvements in acceptance by users et al.)

8) **Principle of user assistance**—Developers should take it into consideration that AI systems will support users and make it possible to give them opportunities for choice in appropriate manners.

9) **Principle of accountability**—Developers should make efforts to fulfill their accountability to stakeholders including AI systems' users.

5. Comments on AI R&D Principles

1) Principle of collaboration—Developers should pay attention to the interconnectivity and interoperability of AI systems.

[Comment]

Developers should give consideration to the interconnectivity and interoperability[6] between the AI systems that they have developed and other AI systems, etc. with consideration of the diversity of AI systems so that: (a) the benefits of AI systems should increase through the sound progress of AI networking; and that (b) multiple developers' efforts to control the risks should be coordinated well and operate effectively. For this, developers should pay attention to the following:

- To make efforts to cooperate to share relevant information which is effective in ensuring interconnectivity and interoperability.

- To make efforts to develop AI systems conforming to international standards, if any.

- To make efforts to address the standardization of data formats and the openness of interfaces and protocols including application programming interface (API).

- To pay attention to risks of unintended events as a result of the interconnection or interoperations between AI systems that they have developed and other AI systems, etc.

- To make efforts to promote open and fair treatment of license agreements for and their conditions of intellectual property rights, such as standard essential patents, contributing to ensuring the interconnectivity and interoperability between AI systems and other AI systems, etc., while taking into consideration the balance between the protection and the utilization with respect to intellectual property related to the development of AI.

2) Principle of transparency—Developers should pay attention to the verifiability of inputs/outputs of AI systems and the explainability of their judgments[7].

[Comment]

AI systems which are supposed to be subject to this principle are such ones that might affect the life, body, freedom, privacy, or property of users or third parties.

---

[6] The interoperability and interconnectivity in this context expects that AI systems which developers have developed can be connected to information-and-communication networks, thereby can operate with other AI systems, etc. in mutually and appropriately harmonized manners.

[7] Note that this principle is not intended to ask developers to disclose algorithms, source codes, or learning data. In interpreting this principle, consideration to privacy and trade secrets is also required.

It is desirable that developers pay attention to the verifiability of the inputs and outputs of AI systems as well as the explainability of the judgment of AI systems within a reasonable scope in light of the characteristics of the technologies to be adopted and their use, so as to obtain the understanding and trust of the society including users of AI systems.

3) Principle of controllability—Developers should pay attention to the controllability of AI systems.

[Comment]

In order to assess the risks related to the controllability of AI systems, it is encouraged that developers make efforts to conduct verification and validation[8] in advance[9]. One of the conceivable methods of risk assessment is to conduct experiments in a closed space such as in a laboratory or a sandbox in which security is ensured, at a stage before the practical application in society.

In addition, in order to ensure the controllability of AI systems, it is encouraged that developers pay attention to whether the supervision (such as monitoring or warnings) and countermeasures (such as system shutdown, cut-off from networks, or repairs) by humans or other trustworthy AI systems are effective, to the extent possible in light of the characteristics of the technologies to be adopted.

4) Principle of safety—Developers should take it into consideration that AI systems will not harm the life, body, or property of users or third parties through actuators or other devices.

[Comment]

AI systems which are supposed to be subject to this principle are such ones that might harm the life, body, or property of users or third parties through actuators or other devices.

---

[8] Verification and validation are methods for evaluating and controlling risks in advance. Generally, the former is used for confirming formal consistency, while the latter is used for confirming substantial validity. (*See, e.g.*, The Future of Life Institute (FLI), *Research Priorities for Robust and Beneficial Artificial Intelligence* (2015)).

[9] Examples of what to see in the risk assessment are risks of *reward hacking* in which AI systems formally achieve the goals assigned but substantially do not meet the developer's intents, and risks that AI systems work in ways that the developers have not intended due to the changes of their outputs and programs in the process of the utilization with their learning, etc. For reward hacking, *see, e.g.*, Dario Amodei, Chris Olah, Jacob Steinhardt, Paul Christiano, John Schulman & Dan Mané, *Concrete Problems in AI Safety*, arXiv: 1606.06565 [cs.AI] (2016).

It is encouraged that developers refer to relevant international standards and pay attention to the followings, with particular consideration of the possibility that outputs or programs might change as a result of learning or other methods of AI systems:

• To make efforts to conduct verification and validation in advance in order to assess and mitigate the risks related to the safety of the AI systems.

• To make efforts to implement measures, throughout the development stage of AI systems to the extent possible in light of the characteristics of the technologies to be adopted, to contribute to the intrinsic safety (reduction of essential risk factors such as kinetic energy of actuators) and the functional safety (mitigation of risks by operation of additional control devices such as automatic braking) when AI systems work with actuators or other devices. And

• To make efforts to explain the designers' intent of AI systems and the reasons for it to stakeholders such as users, when developing AI systems to be used for making judgments regarding the safety of life, body, or property of users and third parties (for example, such judgments that prioritizes life, body, property to be protected at the time of an accident of a robot equipped with AI).

5) Principle of security—Developers should pay attention to the security of AI systems.

[Comment]

In addition to respecting international guidelines on security such as "OECD Guidelines for the Security of Information Systems and Networks," it is encouraged that developers pay attention to the followings, with consideration of the possibility that AI systems might change their outputs or programs as a result of learning or other methods:

• To pay attention, as necessary, to the reliability (that is, whether the operations are performed as intended and not steered by unauthorized third parties) and robustness (that is, tolerance to physical attacks and accidents) of AI systems, in addition to: (a) confidentiality; (b) integrity; and (c) availability of information that are usually required for ensuring the information security of AI systems.

• To make efforts to conduct verification and validation in advance in order to assess and control the risks related to the security of AI systems.

● To make efforts to take measures to maintain the security to the extent possible in light of the characteristics of the technologies to be adopted throughout the process of the development of AI systems ("*security by design*").

6) Principle of privacy—Developers should take it into consideration that AI systems will not infringe the privacy of users or third parties.

[Comment]

The privacy referred to in this principle includes spatial privacy (peace of personal life), information privacy (personal data), and secrecy of communications. Developers should consider international guidelines on privacy, such as "OECD Guidelines on the Protection of Privacy and Transborder Flows of Personal Data," as well as the followings, with consideration of the possibility that AI systems might change their outputs or programs as a result of learning and other methods:

● To make efforts to evaluate the risks of privacy infringement and conduct privacy impact assessment in advance.

● To make efforts to take necessary measures, to the extent possible in light of the characteristics of the technologies to be adopted throughout the process of development of the AI systems ("*privacy by design*"), to avoid infringement of privacy at the time of the utilization.

7) Principle of ethics—Developers should respect human dignity and individual autonomy in the R&D of AI systems.

[Comment]

It is encouraged that, when developing AI systems that link with the human brain and body, developers pay particularly due consideration to respecting human dignity and individual autonomy, in light of discussions on bioethics, etc.

It is also encouraged that, to the extent possible in light of the characteristics of the technologies to be adopted, developers make efforts to take necessary measures so as not to cause unfair discrimination resulting from prejudice included in the learning data of the AI systems.

It is advisable that developers take precautions to ensure that AI systems do not unduly infringe the value of humanity, based on the International Human Rights Law and the International Humanitarian Law.

8) Principle of user assistance—Developers should take it into consideration that AI systems will support users and make it possible to give them opportunities for choice in appropriate manners.

[Comment]

In order to support users of AI systems, it is recommended that developers pay attention to the following:

- To make efforts to make available interfaces that provide in a timely and appropriate manner the information that can help users' decisions and are easy-to-use for them.

- To make efforts to give consideration to make available functions that provide users with opportunities for choice in a timely and appropriate manner (e.g., default settings, easy-to-understand options, feedbacks, emergency warnings, handling of errors, etc.). And

- To make efforts to take measures to make AI systems easier to use for socially-vulnerable people such as universal design.

In addition, it is recommended that developers make efforts to provide users with appropriate information considering the possibility of changes in outputs or programs as a result of learning or other methods of AI systems.

9) Principle of accountability—Developers should make efforts to fulfill their accountability to stakeholders including AI systems' users.

[Comment]

Developers are expected to fulfill their accountability for AI systems they have developed to gain users' trust in AI systems.

Specifically, it is encouraged that developers make efforts to provide users with the information that can help their choice and utilization of AI systems. In addition, in order to improve the acceptance of AI systems by the society including users, it is also encouraged that, taking into account the R&D principles (1) to (8) set forth in the Guidelines, developers make efforts: (a) to provide users et al. with both information and explanations about the technical characteristics of the AI systems they have developed; and (b) to gain active involvement of stakeholders (such as their feedback) in such manners as to hear various views through dialogues with diverse stakeholders.

Moreover, it is advisable that developers make efforts to share the information and cooperate with providers et al. who offer services with the AI systems they have developed on their own.

Attachment: Roles Expected to Be Taken by Related Stakeholders

Based on the purpose of the Guidelines, the stakeholders of relevant industries, academia, and governments are expected to play the following roles, for example:

1. Each country's government and international organizations are expected to make efforts to improve the environment for promoting **dialogues among various stakeholders** such as governments, international organizations, developers, users including civil society, in the operation and review of the Guidelines.

2. Relevant stakeholders such as developers and users including the civil society are expected to make efforts to participate in the dialogues mentioned above, **share best practices** conforming to the Guidelines, and also share common perceptions about the promotion of the benefits and the mitigation of the risks of AI, while ensuring the diversity of discussions over AI.

3. Standardization bodies and other related entities are expected to **prepare and release recommended models** that conform to the Guidelines.

4. Each country's government is expected to: (a) provide assistance **to AI-developer communities** towards solving challenges such as increasing the benefits from AI and mitigating the risks as stated in the Guidelines; and (b) actively **promote policies to support the R&D of AI**.

White House, Executive Order 13859,
Maintaining American Leadership in Artificial Intelligence
(2019)

By the authority vested in me as President by the Constitution and the laws of the United States of America, it is hereby ordered as follows:

<u>Section 1</u>. <u>Policy and Principles</u>. Artificial Intelligence (AI) promises to drive growth of the United States economy, enhance our economic and national security, and improve our quality of life. The United States is the world leader in AI research and development (R&D) and deployment. Continued American leadership in AI is of paramount importance to maintaining the economic and national security of the United States and to shaping the global evolution of AI in a manner consistent with our Nation's values, policies, and priorities. The Federal Government plays an important role in facilitating AI R&D, promoting the trust of the American people in the development and deployment of AI-related technologies, training a workforce capable of using AI in their occupations, and protecting the American AI technology base from attempted acquisition by strategic competitors and adversarial nations. Maintaining American leadership in AI requires a concerted effort to promote advancements in technology and innovation, while protecting American technology, economic and national security, civil liberties, privacy, and American values and enhancing international and industry collaboration with foreign partners and allies. It is the policy of the United States Government to sustain and enhance the scientific, technological, and economic leadership position of the United States in AI R&D and deployment through a coordinated Federal Government strategy, the American AI Initiative (Initiative), guided by five principles:

(a) The United States must drive technological breakthroughs in AI across the Federal Government, industry, and academia in order to promote scientific discovery, economic competitiveness, and national security.

(b) The United States must drive development of appropriate technical standards and reduce barriers to the safe testing and deployment of AI technologies in order to enable the creation of new AI-related industries and the adoption of AI by today's industries.

(c) The United States must train current and future generations of American workers with the skills to develop and apply AI technologies to prepare them for today's economy and jobs of the future.

(d) The United States must foster public trust and confidence in AI technologies and protect civil liberties, privacy, and American values in their application in order to fully realize the potential of AI technologies for the American people.

(e) The United States must promote an international environment that supports American AI research and innovation and opens markets for American AI industries, while protecting our technological advantage in AI and protecting our critical AI technologies from acquisition by strategic competitors and adversarial nations.

Sec. 2. Objectives. Artificial Intelligence will affect the missions of nearly all executive departments and agencies (agencies). Agencies determined to be implementing agencies pursuant to section 3 of this order shall pursue six strategic objectives in furtherance of both promoting and protecting American advancements in AI:

(a) Promote sustained investment in AI R&D in collaboration with industry, academia, international partners and allies, and other non-Federal entities to generate technological breakthroughs in AI and related technologies and to rapidly transition those breakthroughs into capabilities that contribute to our economic and national security.

(b) Enhance access to high-quality and fully traceable Federal data, models, and computing resources to increase the value of such resources for AI R&D, while maintaining safety, security, privacy, and confidentiality protections consistent with applicable laws and policies.

(c) Reduce barriers to the use of AI technologies to promote their innovative application while protecting American technology, economic and national security, civil liberties, privacy, and values.

(d) Ensure that technical standards minimize vulnerability to attacks from malicious actors and reflect Federal priorities for innovation, public trust, and public confidence in systems that use AI technologies; and develop international standards to promote and protect those priorities.

(e) Train the next generation of American AI researchers and users through apprenticeships; skills programs; and education in science, technology, engineering, and mathematics (STEM), with an emphasis on computer science, to ensure that American workers, including Federal workers, are capable of taking full advantage of the opportunities of AI.

(f) Develop and implement an action plan, in accordance with the National Security Presidential Memorandum of February 11, 2019 (Protecting the United

States Advantage in Artificial Intelligence and Related Critical Technologies) (the NSPM) to protect the advantage of the United States in AI and technology critical to United States economic and national security interests against strategic competitors and foreign adversaries.

Sec. 3. <u>Roles and Responsibilities</u>. The Initiative shall be coordinated through the National Science and Technology Council (NSTC) Select Committee on Artificial Intelligence (Select Committee). Actions shall be implemented by agencies that conduct foundational AI R&D, develop and deploy applications of AI technologies, provide educational grants, and regulate and provide guidance for applications of AI technologies, as determined by the co-chairs of the NSTC Select Committee (implementing agencies).

Sec. 4. <u>Federal Investment in AI Research and Development</u>.

(a) Heads of implementing agencies that also perform or fund R&D (AI R&D agencies), shall consider AI as an agency R&D priority, as appropriate to their respective agencies' missions, consistent with applicable law and in accordance with the Office of Management and Budget (OMB) and the Office of Science and Technology Policy (OSTP) R&D priorities memoranda. Heads of such agencies shall take this priority into account when developing budget proposals and planning for the use of funds in Fiscal Year 2020 and in future years. Heads of these agencies shall also consider appropriate administrative actions to increase focus on AI for 2019.

(b) Heads of AI R&D agencies shall budget an amount for AI R&D that is appropriate for this prioritization.

(i) Following the submission of the President's Budget request to the Congress, heads of such agencies shall communicate plans for achieving this prioritization to the OMB Director and the OSTP Director each fiscal year through the Networking and Information Technology Research and Development (NITRD) Program.

(ii) Within 90 days of the enactment of appropriations for their respective agencies, heads of such agencies shall identify each year, consistent with applicable law, the programs to which the AI R&D priority will apply and estimate the total amount of such funds that will be spent on each such program. This information shall be communicated to the OMB Director and OSTP Director each fiscal year through the NITRD Program.

(c) To the extent appropriate and consistent with applicable law, heads of AI R&D agencies shall explore opportunities for collaboration with non-Federal entities, including: the private sector; academia; non-profit organizations; State, local, tribal, and territorial governments; and foreign partners and allies, so all collaborators can benefit from each other's investment and expertise in AI R&D.

Sec. 5. Data and Computing Resources for AI Research and Development.

(a) Heads of all agencies shall review their Federal data and models to identify opportunities to increase access and use by the greater non-Federal AI research community in a manner that benefits that community, while protecting safety, security, privacy, and confidentiality. Specifically, agencies shall improve data and model inventory documentation to enable discovery and usability, and shall prioritize improvements to access and quality of AI data and models based on the AI research community's user feedback.

> (i)   Within 90 days of the date of this order, the OMB Director shall publish a notice in the *Federal Register* inviting the public to identify additional requests for access or quality improvements for Federal data and models that would improve AI R&D and testing. Additionally, within 90 days of the date of this order, OMB, in conjunction with the Select Committee, shall investigate barriers to access or quality limitations of Federal data and models that impede AI R&D and testing. Collectively, these actions by OMB will help to identify datasets that will facilitate non-Federal AI R&D and testing.

> (ii)   Within 120 days of the date of this order, OMB, including through its interagency councils and the Select Committee, shall update implementation guidance for Enterprise Data Inventories and Source Code Inventories to support discovery and usability in AI R&D.

> (iii) Within 180 days of the date of this order, and in accordance with the implementation of the Cross-Agency Priority Goal: Leveraging Federal Data as a Strategic Asset, from the March 2018 President's Management Agenda, agencies shall consider methods of improving the quality, usability, and appropriate access to priority data identified by the AI research community. Agencies shall also identify any associated resource implications.

> (iv)   In identifying data and models for consideration for increased public access, agencies, in coordination with the Senior Agency Officials for Privacy established pursuant to Executive Order 13719 of February 9, 2016 (Establishment of the Federal Privacy Council), the heads of Federal statistical entities, Federal program managers, and other relevant personnel

shall identify any barriers to, or requirements associated with, increased access to and use of such data and models, including:

> (A) privacy and civil liberty protections for individuals who may be affected by increased access and use, as well as confidentiality protections for individuals and other data providers;

> (B) safety and security concerns, including those related to the association or compilation of data and models;

> (C) data documentation and formatting, including the need for interoperable and machine-readable data formats;

> (D) changes necessary to ensure appropriate data and system governance; and

> (E) any other relevant considerations.

(v) In accordance with the President's Management Agenda and the Cross-Agency Priority Goal: Leveraging Data as a Strategic Asset, agencies shall identify opportunities to use new technologies and best practices to increase access to and usability of open data and models, and explore appropriate controls on access to sensitive or restricted data and models, consistent with applicable laws and policies, privacy and confidentiality protections, and civil liberty protections.

(b) The Secretaries of Defense, Commerce, Health and Human Services, and Energy, the Administrator of the National Aeronautics and Space Administration, and the Director of the National Science Foundation shall, to the extent appropriate and consistent with applicable law, prioritize the allocation of high-performance computing resources for AI-related applications through:

> (i) increased assignment of discretionary allocation of resources and resource reserves; or

> (ii) any other appropriate mechanisms.

(c) Within 180 days of the date of this order, the Select Committee, in coordination with the General Services Administration (GSA), shall submit a report to the President making recommendations on better enabling the use of cloud computing resources for federally funded AI R&D.

(d) The Select Committee shall provide technical expertise to the American Technology Council on matters regarding AI and the modernization of Federal technology, data, and the delivery of digital services, as appropriate.

Sec. 6. Guidance for Regulation of AI Applications.

(a) Within 180 days of the date of this order, the OMB Director, in coordination with the OSTP Director, the Director of the Domestic Policy Council, and the Director of the National Economic Council, and in consultation with any other relevant agencies and key stakeholders as the OMB Director shall determine, shall issue a memorandum to the heads of all agencies that shall:

> (i) inform the development of regulatory and non-regulatory approaches by such agencies regarding technologies and industrial sectors that are either empowered or enabled by AI, and that advance American innovation while upholding civil liberties, privacy, and American values; and

> (ii) consider ways to reduce barriers to the use of AI technologies in order to promote their innovative application while protecting civil liberties, privacy, American values, and United States economic and national security.

(b) To help ensure public trust in the development and implementation of AI applications, OMB shall issue a draft version of the memorandum for public comment before it is finalized.

(c) Within 180 days of the date of the memorandum described in subsection (a) of this section, the heads of implementing agencies that also have regulatory authorities shall review their authorities relevant to applications of AI and shall submit to OMB plans to achieve consistency with the memorandum.

(d) Within 180 days of the date of this order, the Secretary of Commerce, through the Director of the National Institute of Standards and Technology (NIST), shall issue a plan for Federal engagement in the development of technical standards and related tools in support of reliable, robust, and trustworthy systems that use AI technologies. NIST shall lead the development of this plan with participation from relevant agencies as the Secretary of Commerce shall determine.

> (i) Consistent with OMB Circular A-119, this plan shall include:

>> (A) Federal priority needs for standardization of AI systems development and deployment;

(B) identification of standards development entities in which Federal agencies should seek membership with the goal of establishing or supporting United States technical leadership roles; and

(C) opportunities for and challenges to United States leadership in standardization related to AI technologies.

(ii) This plan shall be developed in consultation with the Select Committee, as needed, and in consultation with the private sector, academia, non-governmental entities, and other stakeholders, as appropriate.

Sec. 7. AI and the American Workforce.

(a) Heads of implementing agencies that also provide educational grants shall, to the extent consistent with applicable law, consider AI as a priority area within existing Federal fellowship and service programs.

(i) Eligible programs for prioritization shall give preference to American citizens, to the extent permitted by law, and shall include:

(A) high school, undergraduate, and graduate fellowship; alternative education; and training programs;

(B) programs to recognize and fund early-career university faculty who conduct AI R&D, including through Presidential awards and recognitions;

(C) scholarship for service programs;

(D) direct commissioning programs of the United States Armed Forces; and

(E) programs that support the development of instructional programs and curricula that encourage the integration of AI technologies into courses in order to facilitate personalized and adaptive learning experiences for formal and informal education and training.

(ii) Agencies shall annually communicate plans for achieving this prioritization to the co-chairs of the Select Committee.

(b) Within 90 days of the date of this order, the Select Committee shall provide recommendations to the NSTC Committee on STEM Education regarding AI-related educational and workforce development considerations that focus on American citizens.

(c) The Select Committee shall provide technical expertise to the National Council for the American Worker on matters regarding AI and the American workforce, as appropriate.

Sec. 8. Action Plan for Protection of the United States Advantage in AI Technologies.

(a) As directed by the NSPM, the Assistant to the President for National Security Affairs, in coordination with the OSTP Director and the recipients of the NSPM, shall organize the development of an action plan to protect the United States advantage in AI and AI technology critical to United States economic and national security interests against strategic competitors and adversarial nations.

(b) The action plan shall be provided to the President within 120 days of the date of this order, and may be classified in full or in part, as appropriate.

(c) Upon approval by the President, the action plan shall be implemented by all agencies who are recipients of the NSPM, for all AI-related activities, including those conducted pursuant to this order.

Sec. 9. Definitions. As used in this order:

(a) the term "artificial intelligence" means the full extent of Federal investments in AI, to include: R&D of core AI techniques and technologies; AI prototype systems; application and adaptation of AI techniques; architectural and systems support for AI; and cyberinfrastructure, data sets, and standards for AI; and

(b) the term "open data" shall, in accordance with OMB Circular A-130 and memorandum M-13-13, mean "publicly available data structured in a way that enables the data to be fully discoverable and usable by end users."

Sec. 10. General Provisions.

(a) Nothing in this order shall be construed to impair or otherwise affect:

(i) the authority granted by law to an executive department or agency, or the head thereof; or

(ii) the functions of the Director of OMB relating to budgetary, administrative, or legislative proposals.

(b) This order shall be implemented consistent with applicable law and subject to the availability of appropriations.

(c) This order is not intended to, and does not, create any right or benefit, substantive or procedural, enforceable at law or in equity by any party against the United States, its departments, agencies, or entities, its officers, employees, or agents, or any other person.

DONALD J. TRUMP

THE WHITE HOUSE,
February 11, 2019.

Australian Government,
Artificial Intelligence: Australia's Ethics Framework,
A Discussion Paper
(2019)

Core Principles for AI

1. Generates net-benefits. The AI system must generate benefits for people that are greater than the costs.

2. Do no harm. Civilian AI systems must not be designed to harm or deceive people and should be implemented in ways that minimise any negative outcomes.

3. Regulatory and legal compliance. The AI system must comply with all relevant international, Australian Local, State/Territory and Federal government obligations, regulations and laws.

4. Privacy protection. Any system, including AI systems, must ensure people's private data is protected and kept confidential plus prevent data breaches which could cause reputational, psychological, financial, professional or other types of harm.

5. Fairness. The development or use of the AI system must not result in unfair discrimination against individuals, communities or groups. This requires particular attention to ensure the "training data" is free from bias or characteristics which may cause the algorithm to behave unfairly.

6. Transparency & Explainability. People must be informed when an algorithm is being used that impacts them and they should be provided with information about what information the algorithm uses to make decisions.

7. Contestability. When an algorithm impacts a person there must be an efficient process to allow that person to challenge the use or output of the algorithm.

8. Accountability. People and organisations responsible for the creation and implementation of AI algorithms should be identifiable and accountable for the impacts of that algorithm, even if the impacts are unintended.

Canada-France Statement on Artificial Intelligence
(2018)

Canada and France affirm that artificial intelligence is a revolution whose impact is being felt more and more each day. In the near future, it will influence all human activity, providing unprecedented economic and social benefits. Innovations in artificial intelligence technologies will create new sources of economic growth that could make our economies more competitive, inclusive and sustainable, create jobs and shape a better future for all our citizens.

Reaffirming the G7 Innovation Ministers' Statement on Artificial Intelligence adopted in Montréal on March 28, 2018, Canada and France wish to promote a vision of human-centric artificial intelligence grounded in human rights, inclusion, diversity, innovation and economic growth. The widespread use of these new technologies will have a profound effect on everyday life and societal progress, creating both opportunities and challenges.

In this context, Canada and France emphasize the need to develop the capacity to anticipate impacts and coordinate efforts in order to encourage trust and promote the development of artificial intelligence. To this end, we are calling for the creation of an international study group that can become a global point of reference for understanding and sharing research results on artificial intelligence issues and best practices. This initiative will work to create internationally recognized expertise and provide a mechanism for sharing multidisciplinary analysis, foresight and coordination capabilities in the area of artificial intelligence that is inclusive and multistakeholder in its approach.

The group, comprised of government experts, joined by internationally recognized science, industry, and civil society experts, must be able to work independently to analyze the scientific, technical and socioeconomic information that is needed to gain a better understanding of technological developments in artificial intelligence and to identify the consequences of their use. Supported by a small permanent structure, the group will lay the foundation for global collaboration and expertise in the area of artificial intelligence, giving early consideration to impacts on citizens and accelerating the capacity to address opportunities of common interest to our citizens.

Canada and France will set up a task force, which could include other interested parties, in order to make recommendations on the scope, governance and implementation of the international study group. By the end of the year, the task force will submit a report on the implementation of the international study group, whose results will be shared within the G7.

For the Government of Canada
Navdeep Singh BAINS
Minister of Innovation, Science and Economic Development

For the Government of the French Republic
Frédérique VIDAL
Minister of Higher Education, Research and Innovation

Justin Trudeau, Prime Minister of Canada
Mandate for the International Panel on Artificial Intelligence
(2018)

Mission Statement

The mission of the International Panel on Artificial Intelligence (IPAI) will be to support and guide the responsible adoption of AI that is human-centric and grounded in human rights, inclusion, diversity, innovation and economic growth. The International Panel on AI will facilitate international collaboration in a multistakeholder manner with the scientific community, industry, civil society, related international organizations, and governments.

Background — Canada-France Statement on Artificial Intelligence

As announced by Prime Minister Trudeau and President Macron on June 7, 2018, Canada and France wish to promote a vision of human-centric artificial intelligence. To this end, Canada and France are seeking to create an International Panel on AI that can become a global point of reference for understanding and sharing research results on AI issues and best practices, as well as convening international AI initiatives.

Proposed Mandate

By relying on the expertise of the scientific community, industry, civil society and governments, and by providing a mechanism for sharing multidisciplinary analysis, foresight and coordination capabilities in the area of AI, the International Panel on AI will conduct analysis in order to guide AI policy development and the responsible adoption of AI, grounded in human rights. To this end, the International Panel on AI will produce reports and assessments, at the request of its members. It will also establish working group(s) or other multistakeholder mechanisms to, among other things, share information.

In addition to its own work, International Panel on AI will monitor and draw on the work being done domestically and internationally in the area of AI (e.g. countries of the G7 including the European Union, G20, OECD, United Nations). The International Panel on AI will seek to identify gaps, maximise coordination, and facilitate international collaboration. The International Panel on AI will aim to cover the field of AI and its impacts in a global and comprehensive manner by considering the perspectives related to (i) scientific and technological advances, (ii) economic transformation, (iii) respect for human rights, (iv) the collective and society, (v) geopolitical developments, and (vi) cultural diversity.

The areas covered by the mandate of the International Panel on AI will be refined over time and as the field of AI continues to mature.

For illustrative purposes, the themes of the International Panel on AI's activities could include:

- Data Collection and Access

- Data Control and Privacy

- Trust in AI

- Acceptance and Adoption of AI

- Future of Work

- Governance, Laws and Justice

- Responsible AI and Human Rights

- Equity, Responsibility and Public Good

Expert AI Guidelines

Public Voice, Universal Guidelines for AI
(2018)

New developments in Artificial Intelligence are transforming the world, from science and industry to government administration and finance. The rise of AI decision-making also implicates fundamental rights of fairness, accountability, and transparency. Modern data analysis produces significant outcomes that have real life consequences for people in employment, housing, credit, commerce, and criminal sentencing. Many of these techniques are entirely opaque, leaving individuals unaware whether the decisions were accurate, fair, or even about them.

We propose these Universal Guidelines to inform and improve the design and use of AI. The Guidelines are intended to maximize the benefits of AI, to minimize the risk, and to ensure the protection of human rights. These Guidelines should be incorporated into ethical standards, adopted in national law and international agreements, and built into the design of systems. We state clearly that the primary responsibility for AI systems must reside with those institutions that fund, develop, and deploy these systems.

1. **Right to Transparency.** All individuals have the right to know the basis of an AI decision that concerns them. This includes access to the factors, the logic, and techniques that produced the outcome.

2. **Right to Human Determination.** All individuals have the right to a final determination made by a person.

3. **Identification Obligation.** The institution responsible for an AI system must be made known to the public.

4. **Fairness Obligation.** Institutions must ensure that AI systems do not reflect unfair bias or make impermissible discriminatory decisions.

5. **Assessment and Accountability Obligation.** An AI system should be deployed only after an adequate evaluation of its purpose and objectives, its benefits, as well as its risks. Institutions must be responsible for decisions made by an AI system.

6. **Accuracy, Reliability, and Validity Obligations.** Institutions must ensure the accuracy, reliability, and validity of decisions.

7. **Data Quality Obligation.** Institutions must establish data provenance, and assure quality and relevance for the data input into algorithms.

8. **Public Safety Obligation.** Institutions must assess the public safety risks that arise from the deployment of AI systems that direct or control physical devices, and implement safety controls.

9. **Cybersecurity Obligation.** Institutions must secure AI systems against cybersecurity threats.

10. **Prohibition on Secret Profiling.** No institution shall establish or maintain a secret profiling system.

11. **Prohibition on Unitary Scoring.** No national government shall establish or maintain a general-purpose score on its citizens or residents.

12. **Termination Obligation.** An institution that has established an AI system has an affirmative obligation to terminate the system if human control of the system is no longer possible.

Explanatory Memorandum and References

Context

The Universal Guidelines on Artificial Intelligence (UGAI) call attention to the growing challenges of intelligent computational systems and proposes concrete recommendations that can improve and inform their design. At its core, the purpose of the UGAI is to promote transparency and accountability for these systems and to ensure that people retain control over the systems they create. Not all systems fall within the scope of these Guidelines. Our concern is with those systems that impact the rights of people. Above all else, these systems should do no harm.

The declaration is timely. Governments around the world are developing policy proposals and institutions, both public and private, are supporting research and development of "AI." Invariably, there will be an enormous impact on the public, regardless of their participation in the design and development of these systems. And so, the UGAI reflects a public perspective on these challenges.

The UGAI were announced at the 2018 International Data Protection and Privacy Commissioners Conference, among the most significant meetings of technology leaders and data protection experts in history.

The UGAI builds on prior work by scientific societies, think tanks, NGOs, and international organizations. The UGAI incorporates elements of human rights doctrine, data protection law, and ethical guidelines. The Guidelines include several well-established principles for AI governance, and put forward new principles not previously found in similar policy frameworks.

Terminology

The term "Artificial Intelligence" is both broad and imprecise. It includes aspects of machine learning, rule-based decision-making, and other computational techniques. There are also disputes regarding whether Artificial Intelligence is possible. The UGAI simply acknowledges that this term, in common use, covers a wide range of related issues and adopts the term to engage the current debate. There is no attempt here to define its boundaries, other than to assume that AI requires some degree of automated decision-making. The term "Guidelines" follows the practice of policy frameworks that speak primarily to governments and private companies.

The UGAI speaks to the obligations of "institutions" and the rights of "individuals." This follows from the articulation of fair information practices in the data protection field. The UGAI takes the protection of the individual as a fundamental goal. Institutions, public and private, are understood to be those entities that develop and deploy AI systems. The term "institution" was chosen rather than the more familiar "organization" to underscore the permanent, ongoing nature of the obligations set out in the Guidelines. There is one principle that is addressed to "national governments." The reason for this is discussed below.

Application

These Guidelines should be incorporated into ethical standards, adopted in national law and international agreements, and built into the design of systems.

The Principles

The elements of the **Transparency Principle** can be found in several modern privacy laws, including the US Privacy Act, the EU Data Protection Directive, the GDPR, and the Council of Europe Convention 108. The aim of this principle is to enable independent accountability for automated decisions, with a primary emphasis on the right of the individual to know the basis of an adverse determination. In practical terms, it may not be possible for an individual to interpret the basis of a particular decision, but this does not obviate the need to ensure that such an explanation is possible.

The **Right to a Human Determination** reaffirms that individuals and not machines are responsible for automated decision-making. In many instances, such as the operation of an autonomous vehicle, it would not be possible or practical to insert a human decision prior to an automated decision. But the aim remains to ensure accountability. Thus where an automated system fails, this principle should be understood as a requirement that a human assessment of the outcome be made.

Identification Obligation. This principle seeks to address the identification asymmetry that arises in the interaction between individuals and AI systems. An AI system typically knows a great deal about an individual; the individual may not even know the operator of the AI system. The Identification Obligation establishes the foundation of AI accountability which is to make clear the identity of an AI system and the institution responsible.

The **Fairness Obligation** recognizes that all automated systems make decisions that reflect bias and discrimination, but such decisions should not be normatively unfair. There is no simple answer to the question as to what is unfair or impermissible. The evaluation often depends on context. But the Fairness Obligation makes clear that an assessment of objective outcomes alone is not sufficient to evaluate an AI system. Normative consequences must be assessed, including those that preexist or may be amplified by an AI system.

The **Assessment and Accountability Obligation** speaks to the obligation to assess an AI system prior to and during deployment. Regarding assessment, it should be understood that a central purpose of this obligation is to determine whether an AI system should be established. If an assessment reveals substantial risks, such as those suggested by principles concerning Public Safety and Cybersecurity, then the project should not move forward.

The **Accuracy, Reliability, and Validity Obligations** set out key responsibilities associated with the outcome of automated decisions. The terms are intended to be interpreted both independently and jointly.

The **Data Quality Principle** follows from the preceding obligation.

The **Public Safety Obligation** recognizes that AI systems control devices in the physical world. For this reason, institutions must both assess risks and take precautionary measures as appropriate.

The **Cybersecurity Obligation** follows from the Public Safety Obligation and underscores the risk that even well-designed systems may be the target of hostile actors. Those who develop and deploy AI systems must take these risks into account.

The **Prohibition on Secret Profiling** follows from the earlier Identification Obligation. The aim is to avoid the information asymmetry that arises increasingly with AI systems and to ensure the possibility of independent accountability.

The **Prohibition on Unitary Scoring** speaks directly to the risk of a single, multi-purpose number assigned by a government to an individual. In data protection law, universal identifiers that enable the profiling of individuals across are disfavored. These identifiers are often regulated and in some instances prohibited. The concern with universal scoring, described here as "unitary scoring," is even greater. A unitary score reflects not only a unitary profile but also a predetermined outcome across multiple domains of human activity. There is some risk that unitary scores will also emerge in the private sector. Conceivably, such systems could be subject to market competition and government regulations. But there is not even the possibility of counterbalance with unitary scores assigned by government, and therefore they should be prohibited.

The **Termination Obligation** is the ultimate statement of accountability for an AI system. The obligation presumes that systems must remain within human control. If that is no longer possible, the system should be terminated.

Isaac Asimov,
Three Laws of Robotics
(1942)

1. A robot may not injure a human being or, through inaction, allow a human being to come to harm.

2. A robot must obey orders given it by human beings except where such orders would conflict with the First Law.

3. A robot must protect its own existence as long as such protection does not conflict with the First or Second Law.

Future of Life Institute, Asilomar AI Principles (2017)

Artificial intelligence has already provided beneficial tools that are used every day by people around the world. Its continued development, guided by the following principles, will offer amazing opportunities to help and empower people in the decades and centuries ahead.

Research Issues

1) **Research Goal**: The goal of AI research should be to create not undirected intelligence, but beneficial intelligence.

2) **Research Funding**: Investments in AI should be accompanied by funding for research on ensuring its beneficial use, including thorny questions in computer science, economics, law, ethics, and social studies, such as:

- How can we make future AI systems highly robust, so that they do what we want without malfunctioning or getting hacked?

- How can we grow our prosperity through automation while maintaining people's resources and purpose?

- How can we update our legal systems to be more fair and efficient, to keep pace with AI, and to manage the risks associated with AI?

- What set of values should AI be aligned with, and what legal and ethical status should it have?

3) **Science-Policy Link**: There should be constructive and healthy exchange between AI researchers and policy-makers.

4) **Research Culture**: A culture of cooperation, trust, and transparency should be fostered among researchers and developers of AI.

5) **Race Avoidance**: Teams developing AI systems should actively cooperate to avoid corner-cutting on safety standards.

Ethics and Values

6) **Safety**: AI systems should be safe and secure throughout their operational lifetime, and verifiably so where applicable and feasible.

7) **Failure Transparency**: If an AI system causes harm, it should be possible to ascertain why.

8) **Judicial Transparency**: Any involvement by an autonomous system in judicial decision-making should provide a satisfactory explanation auditable by a competent human authority.

9) **Responsibility**: Designers and builders of advanced AI systems are stakeholders in the moral implications of their use, misuse, and actions, with a responsibility and opportunity to shape those implications.

10) **Value Alignment**: Highly autonomous AI systems should be designed so that their goals and behaviors can be assured to align with human values throughout their operation.

11) **Human Values**: AI systems should be designed and operated so as to be compatible with ideals of human dignity, rights, freedoms, and cultural diversity.

12) **Personal Privacy**: People should have the right to access, manage and control the data they generate, given AI systems' power to analyze and utilize that data.

13) **Liberty and Privacy**: The application of AI to personal data must not unreasonably curtail people's real or perceived liberty.

14) **Shared Benefit**: AI technologies should benefit and empower as many people as possible.

15) **Shared Prosperity**: The economic prosperity created by AI should be shared broadly, to benefit all of humanity.

16) **Human Control**: Humans should choose how and whether to delegate decisions to AI systems, to accomplish human-chosen objectives.

17) **Non-subversion**: The power conferred by control of highly advanced AI systems should respect and improve, rather than subvert, the social and civic processes on which the health of society depends.

18) **AI Arms Race**: An arms race in lethal autonomous weapons should be avoided.

Longer-term Issues

19) **Capability Caution**: There being no consensus, we should avoid strong assumptions regarding upper limits on future AI capabilities.

20) **Importance**: Advanced AI could represent a profound change in the history of life on Earth, and should be planned for and managed with commensurate care and resources.

21) **Risks**: Risks posed by AI systems, especially catastrophic or existential risks, must be subject to planning and mitigation efforts commensurate with their expected impact.

22) **Recursive Self-Improvement**: AI systems designed to recursively self-improve or self-replicate in a manner that could lead to rapidly increasing quality or quantity must be subject to strict safety and control measures.

23) **Common Good**: Superintelligence should only be developed in the service of widely shared ethical ideals, and for the benefit of all humanity rather than one state or organization.

Institute of Electrical and Electronics Engineers, Ethically Aligned Design (1st Ed. 2019)

General Principles

The General Principles of Ethically Aligned Design articulate high-level ethical principles that apply to all types of autonomous and intelligent systems (A/IS), regardless of whether they are physical robots, such as care robots or driverless cars, or software systems, such as medical diagnosis systems, intelligent personal assistants, or algorithmic chat bots, in real, virtual, contextual, and mixed-reality environments.

The General Principles define imperatives for the design, development, deployment, adoption, and decommissioning of autonomous and intelligent systems. The Principles consider the role of A/IS creators, i.e., those who design and manufacture, of operators, i.e., those with expertise specific to use of A/IS, other users, and any other stakeholders or affected parties.

We have created these ethical General Principles for A/IS that:

> • Embody the highest ideals of human beneficence within human rights.
>
> • Prioritize benefits to humanity and the natural environment from the use of A/IS over commercial and other considerations. Benefits to humanity and the natural environment should not be at odds—the former depends on the latter. Prioritizing human well-being does not mean degrading the environment.
>
> • Mitigate risks and negative impacts, including misuse, as A/IS evolve as socio-technical systems, in particular by ensuring actions of A/IS are accountable and transparent.

These General Principles are elaborated in subsequent sections of this chapter of Ethically Aligned Design, with specific contextual, cultural, and pragmatic explorations which impact their implementation.

> ...

Principle 1—Human Rights

A/IS shall be created and operated to respect, promote, and protect internationally recognized human rights.

Background

Human benefit is a crucial goal of A/IS, as is respect for human rights set out in works including, but not limited to: The Universal Declaration of Human Rights, the International Covenant on Civil and Political Rights, the Convention on the Rights of the Child, the Convention on the Elimination of all forms of Discrimination against Women, the Convention on the Rights of Persons with Disabilities, and the Geneva Conventions.

Such rights need to be fully taken into consideration by individuals, companies, professional bodies, research institutions, and governments alike to reflect the principle that A/IS should be designed and operated in a way that both respects and fulfills human rights, freedoms, human dignity, and cultural diversity.

While their interpretation may change over time, "human rights", as defined by international law, provide a unilateral basis for creating any A/IS, as these systems affect humans, their emotions, data, or agency. While the direct coding of human rights in A/IS may be difficult or impossible based on contextual use, newer guidelines from The United Nations provide methods to pragmatically implement human rights ideals within business or corporate contexts that could be adapted for engineers and technologists. In this way, technologists can take into account human rights in the way A/IS are developed, operated, tested, and validated. In short, human rights should be part of the ethical risk assessment of A/IS.

Recommendations

To best respect human rights, society must assure the safety and security of A/IS so that they are designed and operated in a way that benefits humans. Specifically:

- Governance frameworks, including standards and regulatory bodies, should be established to oversee processes which ensure that the use of A/IS does not infringe upon human rights, freedoms, dignity, and privacy, and which ensure traceability. This will contribute to building public trust in A/IS.

- A way to translate existing and forthcoming legal obligations into informed policy and technical considerations is needed. Such a method should allow for diverse cultural norms as well as differing legal and regulatory frameworks.

- A/IS should always be subordinate to human judgment and control.

• For the foreseeable future, A/IS should not be granted rights and privileges equal to human rights.

...

Principle 2—Well-being

A/IS creators shall adopt increased human well-being as a primary success criterion for development.

Background

For A/IS technologies to demonstrably advance benefit for humanity, we need to be able to define and measure the benefit we wish to increase. But often the only indicators utilized in determining success for A/IS are avoiding negative unintended consequences and increasing productivity and economic growth for customers and society. Today, these are largely measured by gross domestic product (GDP), profit, or consumption levels.

Well-being, for the purpose of Ethically Aligned Design, is based on the Organization for Economic Co-operation and Development's (OECD) "Guidelines on Measuring Subjective Well-being" perspective that, "Being able to measure people's quality of life is fundamental when assessing the progress of societies." There is now widespread acknowledgement that measuring subjective well-being is an essential part of measuring quality of life alongside other social and economic dimensions as identified within Nassbaum-Sen's capability approach whereby well-being is objectively defined in terms of human capabilities necessary for functioning and flourishing.

Since modern societies will be largely constituted of A/IS users, we believe these considerations to be relevant for A/IS creators.

A/IS technologies can be narrowly conceived from an ethical standpoint. They can be legal, profitable, and safe in their usage, yet not positively contribute to human and environmental well-being. This means technologies created with the best intentions, but without considering well-being, can still have dramatic negative consequences on people's mental health, emotions, sense of themselves, their autonomy, their ability to achieve their goals, and other dimensions of well-being.

Recommendation

A/IS should prioritize human well-being as an outcome in all system designs, using the best available and widely accepted well-being metrics as their reference point.

...

Principle 3—Data Agency

A/IS creators shall empower individuals with the ability to access and securely share their data, to maintain people's capacity to have control over their identity.

Background

Digital consent is a misnomer in its current manifestation. Terms and conditions or privacy policies are largely designed to provide legally accurate information regarding the usage of people's data to safeguard institutional and corporate interests, while often neglecting the needs of the people whose data they process. "Consent fatigue", the constant request for agreement to sets of long and unreadable data handling conditions, causes a majority of users to simply click and accept terms in order to access the services they wish to use. General obfuscation regarding privacy policies, and scenarios like the Cambridge Analytica scandal in 2018, demonstrate that even when individuals provide consent, the understanding of the value regarding their data and its safety is out of an individual's control. T

This existing model of data exchange has eroded human agency in the algorithmic age. People don't know how their data is being used at all times or when predictive messaging is honoring their existing preferences or manipulating them to create new behaviors.

Regulations like the EU General Data Protection Regulation (GDPR) will help improve this lack of clarity regarding the exchange of personal data. But compliance with existing models of consent is not enough to safeguard people's agency regarding their personal information. In an era where A/IS are already pervasive in society, governments must recognize that limiting the misuse of personal data is not enough.

Society must also recognize that human rights in the digital sphere don't exist until individuals globally are empowered with means—including tools and policies—that ensure their dignity through some form of sovereignty, agency, symmetry, or control regarding their identity and personal data. These rights rely on individuals being able to make their choices, outside of the potential influence of biased algorithmic messaging or bad actors. Society also needs to be confident that those who are unable to provide legal informed consent, including minors and people with diminished capacity to make informed decisions, do not lose their dignity due to this.

Recommendation

Organizations, including governments, should immediately explore, test, and implement technologies and policies that let individuals specify their online agent for case-by-case authorization decisions as to who can process what personal data for what purpose. For minors and those with diminished capacity to make informed decisions, current guardianship approaches should be viewed to determine their suitability in this context.

The general solution to give agency to the individual is meant to anticipate and enable individuals to own and fully control autonomous and intelligent (as in capable of learning) technology that can evaluate data use requests by external parties and service providers. This technology would then provide a form of "digital sovereignty" and could issue limited and specific authorizations for processing of the individual's personal data wherever it is held in a compatible system.

...

Principle 4—Effectiveness

Creators and operators shall provide evidence of the effectiveness and fitness for purpose of A/IS.

Background

The responsible adoption and deployment of A/IS are essential if such systems are to realize their many potential benefits to the well-being of both individuals and societies. A/IS will not be trusted unless they can be shown to be effective in use. Harms caused by A/IS, from harm to an individual through to systemic damage, can undermine the perceived value of A/IS and delay or prevent its adoption.

Operators and other users will therefore benefit from measurement of the effectiveness of the A/IS in question. To be adequate, effective measurements need to be both valid and accurate, as well as meaningful and actionable. And such measurements must be accompanied by practical guidance on how to interpret and respond to them.

Recommendations

1. Creators engaged in the development of A/IS should seek to define metrics or benchmarks that will serve as valid and meaningful gauges of the effectiveness of the system in meeting its objectives, adhering to standards and remaining within risk tolerances. Creators building A/IS should ensure that the results when the

defined metrics are applied are readily obtainable by all interested parties, e.g., users, safety certifiers, and regulators of the system.

2. Creators of A/IS should provide guidance on how to interpret and respond to the metrics generated by the systems.

3. To the extent warranted by specific circumstances, operators of A/IS should follow the guidance on measurement provided with the systems, i.e., which metrics to obtain, how and when to obtain them, how to respond to given results, and so on.

4. To the extent that measurements are sample-based, measurements should account for the scope of sampling error, e.g., the reporting of confidence intervals associated with the measurements. Operators should be advised how to interpret the results.

5. Creators of A/IS should design their systems such that metrics on specific deployments of the system can be aggregated to provide information on the effectiveness of the system across multiple deployments. For example, in the case of autonomous vehicles, metrics should be generated both for a specific instance of a vehicle and for a fleet of many instances of the same kind of vehicle.

6. In interpreting and responding to measurements, allowance should be made for variation in the specific objectives and circumstances of a given deployment of A/IS.

7. To the extent possible, industry associations or other organizations, e.g., IEEE and ISO, should work toward developing standards for the measurement and reporting on the effectiveness of A/IS.

...

Principle 5—Transparency

The basis of a particular A/IS decision should always be discoverable.

Background

A key concern over autonomous and intelligent systems is that their operation must be transparent to a wide range of stakeholders for different reasons, noting that the level of transparency will necessarily be different for each stakeholder. Transparent A/IS are ones in which it is possible to discover how and why a system made a particular decision, or in the case of a robot, acted the way it did. The term "transparency" in the context of A/IS also addresses the concepts of traceability, explainability, and interpretability.

A/IS will perform tasks that are far more complex and have more effect on our world than prior generations of technology. Where the task is undertaken in a non-deterministic manner, it may defy simple explanation. This reality will be particularly acute with systems that interact with the physical world, thus raising the potential level of harm that such a system could cause. For example, some A/IS already have real consequences to human safety or well-being, such as medical diagnosis or driverless car autopilots. Systems such as these are safetycritical systems.

At the same time, the complexity of A/IS technology and the non-intuitive way in which it may operate will make it difficult for users of those systems to understand the actions of the A/IS that they use, or with which they interact. This opacity, combined with the often distributed manner in which the A/IS are developed, will complicate efforts to determine and allocate responsibility when something goes wrong. Thus, lack of transparency increases the risk and magnitude of harm when users do not understand the systems they are using, or there is a failure to fix faults and improve systems following accidents. Lack of transparency also increases the difficulty of ensuring accountability (see Principle 6— Accountability).

Achieving transparency, which may involve a significant portion of the resources required to develop the A/IS, is important to each stakeholder group for the following reasons:

1. For users, what the system is doing and why.

2. For creators, including those undertaking the validation and certification of A/IS, the systems' processes and input data.

3. For an accident investigator, if accidents occur.

4. For those in the legal process, to inform evidence and decision-making.

5. For the public, to build confidence in the technology

Recommendation

Develop new standards that describe measurable, testable levels of transparency, so that systems can be objectively assessed and levels of compliance determined. For designers, such standards will provide a guide for self-assessing transparency during development and suggest mechanisms for improving transparency. The mechanisms by which transparency is provided will vary significantly, including but not limited to, the following use cases:

1. For users of care or domestic robots, a "why did-you-do-that button" which, when pressed, causes the robot to explain the action it just took.

2. For validation or certification agencies, the algorithms underlying the A/IS and how they have been verified.

3. For accident investigators, secure storage of sensor and internal state data comparable to a flight data recorder or black box.

...

Principle 6 — Accountability

A/IS shall be created and operated to provide an unambiguous rationale for decisions made.

Background

The programming, output, and purpose of A/IS are often not discernible by the general public. Based on the cultural context, application, and use of A/IS, people and institutions need clarity around the manufacture and deployment of these systems to establish responsibility and accountability, and to avoid potential harm. Additionally, manufacturers of these systems must be accountable in order to address legal issues of culpability. It should, if necessary, be possible to apportion culpability among responsible creators (designers and manufacturers) and operators to avoid confusion or fear within the general public.

Accountability and partial accountability are not possible without transparency, thus this principle is closely linked with Principle 5–Transparency.

Recommendations

To best address issues of responsibility and accountability:

1. Legislatures/courts should clarify responsibility, culpability, liability, and accountability for A/IS, where possible, prior to development and deployment so that manufacturers and users understand their rights and obligations.

2. Designers and developers of A/IS should remain aware of, and take into account, the diversity of existing cultural norms among the groups of users of these A/IS.

3. Multi-stakeholder ecosystems including creators, and government, civil, and commercial stakeholders, should be developed to help establish norms where they do not exist because A/IS-oriented technology and their impacts are too new. These

ecosystems would include, but not be limited to, representatives of civil society, law enforcement, insurers, investors, manufacturers, engineers, lawyers, and users. The norms can mature into best practices and laws.

4. Systems for registration and record-keeping should be established so that it is always possible to find out who is legally responsible for a particular A/IS. Creators, including manufacturers, along with operators, of A/IS should register key, high-level parameters, including:

- Intended use,

- Training data and training environment, if applicable,

- Sensors and real world data sources,

- Algorithms,

- Process graphs,

- Model features, at various levels,

- User interfaces,

- Actuators and outputs, and

- Optimization goals, loss functions, and reward functions.

      …

Principle 7—Awareness of Misuse

Creators shall guard against all potential misuses and risks of A/IS in operation.

Background

New technologies give rise to greater risk of deliberate or accidental misuse, and this is especially true for A/IS. A/IS increases the impact of risks such as hacking, misuse of personal data, system manipulation, or exploitation of vulnerable users by unscrupulous parties. Cases of A/IS hacking have already been widely reported, with driverless cars, for example. The Microsoft Tay AI chatbot was famously manipulated when it mimicked deliberately offensive users. In an age where these powerful tools are easily available, there is a need for a new kind of education for citizens to be sensitized to risks associated with the misuse of A/IS. The EU's

General Data Protection Regulation (GDPR) provides measures to remedy the misuse of personal data.

Responsible innovation requires A/IS creators to anticipate, reflect, and engage with users of A/IS. Thus, citizens, lawyers, governments, etc., all have a role to play through education and awareness in developing accountability structures (see Principle 6), in addition to guiding new technology proactively toward beneficial ends.

Recommendations

1. Creators should be aware of methods of misuse, and they should design A/IS in ways to minimize the opportunity for these.

2. Raise public awareness around the issues of potential A/IS technology misuse in an informed and measured way by:

> • Providing ethics education and security awareness that sensitizes society to the potential risks of misuse of A/IS. For example, provide "data privacy warnings" that some smart devices will collect their users' personal data.

> • Delivering this education in scalable and effective ways, including having experts with the greatest credibility and impact who can minimize unwarranted fear about A/IS.

> • Educating government, lawmakers, and enforcement agencies about these issues of A/IS so citizens can work collaboratively with these agencies to understand safe use of A/IS. For example, the same way police officers give public safety lectures in schools, they could provide workshops on safe use and interaction with A/IS.

> . . .

Principle 8—Competence

Creators shall specify and operators shall adhere to the knowledge and skill required for safe and effective operation.

Background

A/IS can and often do make decisions that previously required human knowledge, expertise, and reason. Algorithms potentially can make even better decisions, by accessing more information, more quickly, and without the error, inconsistency, and bias that can plague human decision-making. As the use of algorithms becomes common and the decisions they make become more complex, however, the more normal and natural such decisions appear.

Operators of A/IS can become less likely to question and potentially less able to question the decisions that algorithms make. Operators will not necessarily know the sources, scale, accuracy, and uncertainty that are implicit in applications of A/IS. As the use of A/IS expands, more systems will rely on machine learning where actions are not preprogrammed and that might not leave a clear record of the steps that led the system to its current state. Even if those records do exist, operators might not have access to them or the expertise necessary to decipher those records.

Standards for the operators are essential. Operators should be able to understand how A/IS reach their decisions, the information and logic on which the A/IS rely, and the effects of those decisions. Even more crucially, operators should know when they need to question A/IS and when they need to overrule them.

Creators of A/IS should take an active role in ensuring that operators of their technologies have the knowledge, experience, and skill necessary not only to use A/IS, but also to use it safely and appropriately, towards their intended ends. Creators should make provisions for the operators to override A/IS in appropriate circumstances.

While standards for operator competence are necessary to ensure the effective, safe, and ethical application of A/IS, these standards are not the same for all forms of A/IS. The level of competence required for the safe and effective operation of A/IS will range from elementary, such as "intuitive" use guided by design, to advanced, such as fluency in statistics.

Recommendations

1. Creators of A/IS should specify the types and levels of knowledge necessary to understand and operate any given application of A/IS. In specifying the requisite types and levels of expertise, creators should do so for the individual components of A/IS and for the entire systems.

2. Creators of A/IS should integrate safeguards against the incompetent operation of their systems. Safeguards could include issuing notifications/warnings to operators in certain conditions, limiting functionalities for different levels of operators (e.g., novice vs. advanced), system shut-down in potentially risky conditions, etc.

3. Creators of A/IS should provide the parties affected by the output of A/IS with information on the role of the operator, the competencies required, and the implications of operator error. Such documentation should be accessible and understandable to both experts and the general public.

4. Entities that operate A/IS should create documented policies to govern how A/IS should be operated. These policies should include the real-world applications for such A/IS, any preconditions for their effective use, who is qualified to operate them, what training is required for operators, how to measure the performance of the A/IS, and what should be expected from the A/IS. The policies should also include specification of circumstances in which it might be necessary for the operator to override the A/IS.

5. Operators of A/IS should, before operating a system, make sure that they have access to the requisite competencies. The operator need not be an expert in all the pertinent domains but should have access to individuals with the requisite kinds of expertise.

...

Association for Computing Machinery, Statement on Algorithmic Transparency and Accountability (2017)

Computer algorithms are widely employed throughout our economy and society to make decisions that have far-reaching impacts, including their applications for education, access to credit, healthcare, and employment.[1] The ubiquity of algorithms in our everyday lives is an important reason to focus on addressing challenges associated with the design and technical aspects of algorithms and preventing bias from the onset.

An algorithm is a self-contained step-by-step set of operations that computers and other 'smart' devices carry out to perform calculation, data processing, and automated reasoning tasks. Increasingly, algorithms implement institutional decision-making based on analytics, which involves the discovery, interpretation, and communication of meaningful patterns in data. Especially valuable in areas rich with recorded information, analytics relies on the simultaneous application of statistics, computer programming, and operations research to quantify performance.

There is also growing evidence that some algorithms and analytics can be opaque, making it impossible to determine when their outputs may be biased or erroneous.

Computational models can be distorted as a result of biases contained in their input data and/or their algorithms. Decisions made by predictive algorithms can be opaque because of many factors, including technical (the algorithm may not lend itself to easy explanation), economic (the cost of providing transparency may be excessive, including the compromise of trade secrets), and social (revealing input may violate privacy expectations). Even well-engineered computer systems can result in unexplained outcomes or errors, either because they contain bugs or because the conditions of their use changes, invalidating assumptions on which the original analytics were based.

The use of algorithms for automated decision-making about individuals can result in harmful discrimination. Policymakers should hold institutions using analytics to the same standards as institutions where humans have traditionally made decisions

---

[1] Federal Trade Commission. "Big Data: A Tool for Inclusion or Exclusion? Understanding the Issues." January 2016. https://www.ftc.gov/reports/big-data-tool-inclusion-or-exclusion-understanding-issues-ftc-report.

and developers should plan and architect analytical systems to adhere to those standards when algorithms are used to make automated decisions or as input to decisions made by people.

This set of principles, consistent with the ACM Code of Ethics, is intended to support the benefits of algorithmic decision-making while addressing these concerns. These principles should be addressed during every phase of system development and deployment to the extent necessary to minimize potential harms while realizing the benefits of algorithmic decision-making.

Principles for Algorithmic Transparency and Accountability

1. **Awareness**: Owners, designers, builders, users, and other stakeholders of analytic systems should be aware of the possible biases involved in their design, implementation, and use and the potential harm that biases can cause to individuals and society.

2. **Access and redress**: Regulators should encourage the adoption of mechanisms that enable questioning and redress for individuals and groups that are adversely affected by algorithmically informed decisions.

3. **Accountability**: Institutions should be held responsible for decisions made by the algorithms that they use, even if it is not feasible to explain in detail how the algorithms produce their results.

4. **Explanation**: Systems and institutions that use algorithmic decision-making are encouraged to produce explanations regarding both the procedures followed by the algorithm and the specific decisions that are made. This is particularly important in public policy contexts.

5. **Data Provenance**: A description of the way in which the training data was collected should be maintained by the builders of the algorithms, accompanied by an exploration of the potential biases induced by the human or algorithmic data-gathering process. Public scrutiny of the data provides maximum opportunity for corrections. However, concerns over privacy, protecting trade secrets, or revelation of analytics that might allow malicious actors to game the system can justify restricting access to qualified and authorized individuals.

6. **Auditability**: Models, algorithms, data, and decisions should be recorded so that they can be audited in cases where harm is suspected.

7. **Validation and Testing**: Institutions should use rigorous methods to validate their models and document those methods and results. In particular, they should

routinely perform tests to assess and determine whether the model generates discriminatory harm. Institutions are encouraged to make the results of such tests public.

Amnesty International & Access Now,
The Toronto Declaration: Protecting the right to equality and non-discrimination in machine learning systems (2018)

Preamble

1. As machine learning systems advance in capability and increase in use, we must examine the impact of this technology on human rights. We acknowledge the potential for machine learning and related systems to be used to promote human rights, but are increasingly concerned about the capability of such systems to facilitate intentional or inadvertent discrimination against certain individuals or groups of people. We must urgently address how these technologies will affect people and their rights. In a world of machine learning systems, who will bear accountability for harming human rights?

2. As discourse around ethics and artificial intelligence continues, this Declaration aims to draw attention to the relevant and well-established framework of international human rights law and standards. These universal, binding and actionable laws and standards provide tangible means to protect individuals from discrimination, to promote inclusion, diversity and equity, and to safeguard equality. Human rights are "universal, indivisible and interdependent and interrelated."[43]

3. This Declaration aims to build on existing discussions, principles and papers exploring the harms arising from this technology. The significant work done in this area by many experts has helped raise awareness of and inform discussions about the discriminatory risks of machine learning systems.[44] We wish to complement this existing work by reaffirming the role of human rights law and standards in protecting individuals and

---

[43] UN Human Rights Committee, Vienna Declaration and Programme of Action, 1993, http://www.ohchr.org/EN/ProfessionalInterest/Pages/Vienna.aspx

[44] For example, see the FAT/ML *Principles for Accountable Algorithms and a Social Impact Statement for Algorithms*; IEEE Global Initiative on Ethics of Autonomous and Intelligent Systems, *Ethically Aligned Design*; *The Montreal Declaration for a Responsible Development of Artificial Intelligence*; The Asilomar AI Principles, developed by the Future of Life Institute.

groups from discrimination in any context. The human rights law and standards referenced in this Declaration provide solid foundations for developing ethical frameworks for machine learning, including provisions for accountability and means for remedy.

4. From policing, to welfare systems, to healthcare provision, to platforms for online discourse – to name a few examples – systems employing machine learning technologies can vastly and rapidly reinforce or change power structures on an unprecedented scale and with significant harm to human rights, notably the right to equality. There is a substantive and growing body of evidence to show that machine learning systems, which can be opaque and include unexplainable processes, can contribute to discriminatory or otherwise repressive practices if adopted and implemented without necessary safeguards.

5. States and private sector actors should promote the development and use of machine learning and related technologies where they help people exercise and enjoy their human rights. For example, in healthcare, machine learning systems could bring advances in diagnostics and treatments, while potentially making healthcare services more widely available and accessible. In relation to machine learning and artificial intelligence systems more broadly, states should promote the positive right to the enjoyment of developments in science and technology as an affirmation of economic, social and cultural rights.[45]

6. We focus in this Declaration on the right to equality and non-discrimination. There are numerous other human rights that may be adversely affected through the use and misuse of machine learning systems, including the right to privacy and data protection, the right to freedom of expression and association, to participation in cultural life, equality before the law, and access to effective remedy. Systems that make decisions and process data can also undermine economic, social, and cultural rights; for example, they can impact the provision of vital services, such as healthcare and education, and limit access to opportunities like employment.

---

[45] The International Covenant on Economic, Social and Cultural Rights (ICESCR), Article 15 https://www.ohchr.org/EN/ProfessionalInterest/Pages/CESCR.aspx

7. While this Declaration is focused on machine learning technologies, many of the norms and principles included here are equally applicable to technologies housed under the broader term of artificial intelligence, as well as to related data systems.

...

Using the framework of international human rights law

8. **States have obligations to promote, protect and respect human rights; private sector actors, including companies, have a responsibility to respect human rights at all times. We put forward this Declaration to affirm these obligations and responsibilities.**

9. There are many discussions taking place now at supranational, state and regional level, in technology companies, at academic institutions, in civil society and beyond, focusing on the ethics of artificial intelligence and how to make technology in this field human-centric. These issues must be analyzed through a human rights lens to assess current and future potential human rights harms created or facilitated by this technology, and to take concrete steps to address any risk of harm.

10. Human rights law is a universally ascribed system of values based on the rule of law. It provides established means to ensure that rights are upheld, including the rights to equality and non-discrimination. Its nature as a universally binding, actionable set of standards is particularly well-suited for borderless technologies. Human rights law sets standards and provides mechanisms to hold public and private sector actors accountable where they fail to fulfil their respective obligations and responsibilities to protect and respect rights. It also requires that everyone must be able to obtain effective remedy and redress where their rights have been denied or violated.

11. The risks that machine learning systems pose must be urgently examined and addressed at governmental level and by private sector actors who are conceiving, developing and deploying these systems. It is critical that potential harms are identified and addressed and that mechanisms are put in place to hold those responsible for harms to account. Government measures should be binding and adequate to protect and promote rights. Academic, legal and civil society experts should be

able to meaningfully participate in these discussions, and critique and advise on the use of these technologies.

The right to equality and non-discrimination

12. **This Declaration focuses on the right to equality and non-discrimination, a critical principle that underpins all human rights.**

13. Discrimination is defined under international law as "any distinction, exclusion, restriction or preference which is based on any ground such as race, colour, sex, language, religion, political or other opinion, national or social origin, property, birth or other status, and which has the purpose or effect of nullifying or impairing the recognition, enjoyment or exercise by all persons, on an equal footing, of all rights and freedoms."[46] This list is non-exhaustive as the United Nations High Commissioner for Human Rights has recognized the necessity of preventing discrimination against additional classes.[47]

Preventing discrimination

14. **Governments have obligations and private sector actors have responsibilities to proactively prevent discrimination in order to comply with existing human rights law and standards. When prevention is not sufficient or satisfactory, and discrimination arises, a system should be interrogated and harms addressed immediately.**

15. In employing new technologies, both state and private sector actors will likely need to find new ways to protect human rights, as new challenges to equality and representation of and impact on diverse individuals and groups arise.

16. Existing patterns of structural discrimination may be reproduced and aggravated in situations that are particular to these technologies – for example, machine learning system goals that create self-fulfilling

---

[46] United Nations Human Rights Committee, General comment No. 18, UN Doc. RI/GEN/1/Rev.9 Vol. I (1989), para. 7

[47] UN OHCHR, *Tackling Discrimination against Lesbian, Gay, Bi, Trans, & Intersex People Standards of Conduct for Business*, https://www.unfe.org/standards/

markers of success and reinforce patterns of inequality, or issues arising from using non-representative or biased datasets.

17. All actors, public and private, must prevent and mitigate against discrimination risks in the design, development and application of machine learning technologies. They must also ensure that there are mechanisms allowing for access to effective remedy in place before deployment and throughout a system's lifecycle.

Protecting the rights of all individuals and groups: promoting diversity and inclusion

18. This Declaration underlines that inclusion, diversity and equity are key components of protecting and upholding the right to equality and non-discrimination. All must be considered in the development and deployment of machine learning systems in order to prevent discrimination, particularly against marginalised groups.

19. While the collection of data can help mitigate discrimination, there are some groups for whom collecting data on discrimination poses particular difficulty. Additional protections must extend to those groups, including protections for sensitive data.

20. Implicit and inadvertent bias through design creates another means for discrimination, where the conception, development and end use of machine learning systems is largely overseen by a particular sector of society. This technology is at present largely developed, applied and reviewed by companies based in certain countries and regions; the people behind the technology bring their own biases, and are likely to have limited input from diverse groups in terms of race, culture, gender, and socio-economic backgrounds.

21. Inclusion, diversity and equity entails the active participation of, and meaningful consultation with, a diverse community, including end users, during the design and application of machine learning systems, to help ensure that systems are created and used in ways that respect rights – particularly the rights of marginalised groups who are vulnerable to discrimination.

Duties of states: human rights obligations

22. States bear the primary duty to promote, protect, respect and fulfil human rights. Under international law, states must not engage in, or support discriminatory or otherwise rights-violating actions or practices when designing or implementing machine learning systems in a public context or through public-private partnerships.

23. States must adhere to relevant national and international laws and regulations that codify and implement human rights obligations protecting against discrimination and other related rights harms, for example data protection and privacy laws.

24. States have positive obligations to protect against discrimination by private sector actors and promote equality and other rights, including through binding laws.

25. The state obligations outlined in this section also apply to public use of machine learning in partnerships with private sector actors.

State use of machine learning systems

26. **States must ensure that existing measures to prevent against discrimination and other rights harms are updated to take into account and address the risks posed by machine learning technologies.**

27. Machine learning systems are increasingly being deployed or implemented by public authorities in areas that are fundamental to the exercise and enjoyment of human rights, rule of law, due process, freedom of expression, criminal justice, healthcare, access to social welfare benefits, and housing. While this technology may offer benefits in such contexts, there may also be a high risk of discriminatory or other rights-harming outcomes. It is critical that states provide meaningful opportunities for effective remediation and redress of harms where they do occur.

28. As confirmed by the Human Rights Committee, Article 26 of the International Covenant on Civil and Political Rights "prohibits discrimination in law or in fact in any field regulated and protected by public authorities".[48] This is further set out in treaties dealing with

---

[48] United Nations Human Rights Committee, General comment No. 18 (1989), para. 12

specific forms of discrimination, in which states have committed to refrain from engaging in discrimination, and to ensure that public authorities and institutions "act in conformity with this obligation".[49]

29. States must refrain altogether from using or requiring the private sector to use tools that discriminate, lead to discriminatory outcomes, or otherwise harm human rights.

30. **States must take the following steps to mitigate and reduce the harms of discrimination from machine learning in public sector systems:**

i. Identify risks

31. Any state deploying machine learning technologies must thoroughly investigate systems for discrimination and other rights risks prior to development or acquisition, where possible, prior to use, and on an ongoing basis throughout the lifecycle of the technologies, in the contexts in which they are deployed. This may include:

> a) Conducting regular impact assessments prior to public procurement, during development, at regular milestones and throughout the deployment and use of machine learning systems to identify potential sources of discriminatory or other rights-harming outcomes – for example, in algorithmic model design, in oversight processes, or in data processing.[50]

> b) Taking appropriate measures to mitigate risks identified through impact assessments – for example, mitigating inadvertent discrimination or underrepresentation in data or systems; conducting dynamic testing methods and pre-release trials;

---

[49] For example, Convention on the Elimination of All Forms of Racial Discrimination, Article 2 (a), and Convention on the Elimination of All Forms of Discrimination against Women, Article 2(d).

[50] The AI Now Institute has outlined a practical framework for algorithmic impact assessments by public agencies, https://ainowinstitute.org/aiareport2018.pdf. Article 35 of the EU's General Data Protection Regulation (GDPR) sets out a requirement to carry out a Data Protection Impact Assessment (DPIA); in addition, Article 25 of the GDPR requires data protection principles to be applied by design and by default from the conception phase of a product, service or service and through its lifecycle.

ensuring that potentially affected groups and field experts are included as actors with decision-making power in the design, testing and review phases; submitting systems for independent expert review where appropriate.

c) Subjecting systems to live, regular tests and audits; interrogating markers of success for bias and self-fulfilling feedback loops; and ensuring holistic independent reviews of systems in the context of human rights harms in a live environment.

d) Disclosing known limitations of the system in question - for example, noting measures of confidence, known failure scenarios and appropriate limitations of use.

ii. Ensure transparency and accountability

32. States must ensure and require accountability and maximum possible transparency around public sector use of machine learning systems. This must include explainability and intelligibility in the use of these technologies so that the impact on affected individuals and groups can be effectively scrutinised by independent entities, responsibilities established, and actors held to account. States should:

a) Publicly disclose where machine learning systems are used in the public sphere, provide information that explains in clear and accessible terms how automated and machine learning decision-making processes are reached, and document actions taken to identify, document and mitigate against discriminatory or other rights-harming impacts.

b) Enable independent analysis and oversight by using systems that are auditable.

c) Avoid using 'black box systems' that cannot be subjected to meaningful standards of accountability and transparency, and refrain from using these systems at all in high-risk contexts.[51]

---

[51] The AI Now Institute at New York University, *AI Now 2017 Report*, 2017, https://ainowinstitute.org/AI_Now_2017_Report.pdf

iii. Enforce oversight

33. States must take steps to ensure public officials are aware of and sensitive to the risks of discrimination and other rights harms in machine learning systems. States should:

> a) Proactively adopt diverse hiring practices and engage in consultations to assure diverse perspectives so that those involved in the design, implementation, and review of machine learning represent a range of backgrounds and identities.
>
> b) Ensure that public bodies carry out training in human rights and data analysis for officials involved in the procurement, development, use and review of machine learning tools.
>
> c) Create mechanisms for independent oversight, including by judicial authorities when necessary.
>
> d) Ensure that machine learning-supported decisions meet international accepted standards for due process.

34. As research and development of machine learning systems is largely driven by the private sector, in practice states often rely on private contractors to design and implement these technologies in a public context. In such cases, states must not relinquish their own obligations around preventing discrimination and ensuring accountability and redress for human rights harms in the delivery of services.

35. Any state authority procuring machine learning technologies from the private sector should maintain relevant oversight and control over the use of the system, and require the third party to carry out human rights due diligence to identify, prevent and mitigate against discrimination and other human rights harms, and publicly account for their efforts in this regard.

Promoting equality

36. **States have a duty to take proactive measures to eliminate discrimination.**[52]

37. In the context of machine learning and wider technology developments, one of the most important priorities for states is to promote programs that increase diversity, inclusion and equity in the science, technology, engineering and mathematics sectors (commonly referred to as STEM fields). Such efforts do not serve as ends in themselves, though they may help mitigate against discriminatory outcomes. States should also invest in research into ways to mitigate human rights harms in machine learning systems.

Holding private sector actors to account

38. **International law clearly sets out the duty of states to protect human rights; this includes ensuring the right to non-discrimination by private sector actors.**

39. According to the UN Committee on Economic, Social and Cultural Rights, "States parties must therefore adopt measures, which should include legislation, to ensure that individuals and entities in the private sphere do not discriminate on prohibited grounds".[53]

40. States should put in place regulation compliant with human rights law for oversight of the use of machine learning by the private sector in contexts that present risk of discriminatory or other rights-harming outcomes, recognising technical standards may be complementary to regulation. In addition, non-discrimination, data protection, privacy and other areas of law at national and regional levels may expand upon and reinforce international human rights obligations applicable to machine learning.

---

[52] The UN Committee on Economic, Social and Cultural Rights affirms that in addition to refraining from discriminatory actions, "State parties should take concrete, deliberate and targeted measures to ensure that discrimination in the exercise of Covenant rights is eliminated." – UN

[53] UN Committee on Economic, Social and Cultural Rights, General Comment 20, UN Doc. E/C.12/GC/20 (2009) para. 11

41. States must guarantee access to effective remedy for all individuals whose rights are violated or abused through use of these technologies.

Responsibilities of private sector actors: human rights due diligence

42. Private sector actors have a responsibility to respect human rights; this responsibility exists independently of state obligations.[54] As part of fulfilling this responsibility, private sector actors need to take ongoing proactive and reactive steps to ensure that they do not cause or contribute to human rights abuses – a process called 'human rights due diligence'.[55]

43. Private sector actors that develop and deploy machine learning systems should follow a human rights due diligence framework to avoid fostering or entrenching discrimination and to respect human rights more broadly through the use of their systems.

44. There are three core steps to the process of human rights due diligence:

> i. Identify potential discriminatory outcomes

> ii. Take effective action to prevent and mitigate discrimination and track responses

> iii. Be transparent about efforts to identify, prevent and mitigate against discrimination in machine learning systems.

i. Identify potential discriminatory outcomes

45. During the development and deployment of any new machine learning technologies, non-state and private sector actors should assess the risk that the system will result in discrimination. The risk of discrimination and the harms will not be equal in all applications, and the actions required to address discrimination will depend on the context. Actors must be careful to identify not only direct discrimination, but also

---

[54] See UN Guiding Principles on Business and Human Rights and additional supporting documents

[55] See Council of Europe's Recommendation CM/Rec(2018)2 of the Committee of Ministers to member States on the roles and responsibilities of internet intermediaries, https://search.coe.int/cm/Pages/result_details.aspx?ObjectID=0900001680790e14

indirect forms of differential treatment which may appear neutral at face value, but lead to discrimination.

46. When mapping risks, private sector actors should take into account risks commonly associated with machine learning systems – for example, training systems on incomplete or unrepresentative data, or datasets representing historic or systemic bias. Private actors should consult with relevant stakeholders in an inclusive manner, including affected groups, organizations that work on human rights, equality and discrimination, as well as independent human rights and machine learning experts.

ii. Take effective action to prevent and mitigate discrimination and track responses

47. After identifying human rights risks, the second step is to prevent those risks. For developers of machine learning systems, this requires:

> a) Correcting for discrimination, both in the design of the model and the impact of the system and in deciding which training data to use.

> b) Pursuing diversity, equity and other means of inclusion in machine learning development teams, with the aim of identifying bias by design and preventing inadvertent discrimination.

> c) Submitting systems that have a significant risk of resulting in human rights abuses to independent third-party audits.

48. Where the risk of discrimination or other rights violations has been assessed to be too high or impossible to mitigate, private sector actors should not deploy a machine learning system in that context.

49. Another vital element of this step is for private sector actors to track their response to issues that emerge during implementation and over time, including evaluation of the effectiveness of responses. This requires regular, ongoing quality assurances checks and real-time auditing through design, testing and deployment stages to monitor a system for discriminatory impacts in context and situ, and to correct errors and harms as appropriate. This is particularly important given the risk of feedback loops that can exacerbate and entrench discriminatory outcomes.

iii. Be transparent about efforts to identify, prevent and mitigate against discrimination in machine learning systems

50. Transparency is a key component of human rights due diligence, and involves "communication, providing a measure of transparency and accountability to individuals or groups who may be impacted and to other relevant stakeholders."[56]

51. Private sector actors that develop and implement machine learning systems should disclose the process of identifying risks, the risks that have been identified, and the concrete steps taken to prevent and mitigate identified human rights risks. This may include:

> a) Disclosing information about the risks and specific instances of discrimination the company has identified, for example risks associated with the way a particular machine learning system is designed, or with the use of machine learning systems in particular contexts.

> b) In instances where there is a risk of discrimination, publishing technical specification with details of the machine learning and its functions, including samples of the training data used and details of the source of data.

> c) Establishing mechanisms to ensure that where discrimination has occurred through the use of a machine learning system, relevant parties, including affected individuals, are informed of the harms and how they can challenge a decision or outcome.

The right to an effective remedy

---

[56] UN Guiding Principles on Business and Human Rights, Principle 21

52. The right to justice is a vital element of international human rights law.[57] Under international law, victims of human rights violations or abuses must have access to prompt and effective remedies, and those responsible for the violations must be held to account.

53. Companies and private sector actors designing and implementing machine learning systems should take action to ensure individuals and groups have access to meaningful, effective remedy and redress. This may include, for example, creating clear, independent, visible processes for redress following adverse individual or societal effects, and designating roles in the entity responsible for the timely remedy of such issues subject to accessible and effective appeal and judicial review.

54. The use of machine learning systems where people's rights are at stake may pose challenges for ensuring the right to remedy. The opacity of some systems means individuals may be unaware how decisions which affect their rights were made, and whether the process was discriminatory. In some cases, the public body or private sector actors involved may itself be unable to explain the decision-making process.

55. The challenges are particularly acute when machine learning systems that recommend, make or enforce decisions are used within the justice system, the very institutions which are responsible for guaranteeing rights, including the right to access to effective remedy.

56. The measures already outlined around identifying, documenting, and responding to discrimination, and being transparent and accountable about these efforts, will help states to ensure that individuals have access to effective remedies. In addition, states should:

---

[57] For example, see: Universal Declaration of Human Rights, Article 8; International Covenant on Civil and Political Rights, Article 2 (3); International Covenant on Economic, Social and Cultural Rights, Article 2; Committee on Economic, Social and Cultural Rights, General Comment No. 3: The Nature of States Parties' Obligations, UN Doc. E/1991/23 (1990) Article 2 Para. 1 of the Covenant; International Convention on the Elimination of All Forms of Racial Discrimination, Article 6; Convention on the Elimination of All Forms of Discrimination against Women and UN Committee on Economic, Social and Cultural Rights (CESCR), Article 2, General Comment No. 9: The domestic application of the Covenant, E/C.12/1998/24 (1998) http://www.refworld.org/docid/47a7079d6.html

a) Ensure that if machine learning systems are to be deployed in the public sector, use is carried out in line with standards of due process.

b) Act cautiously on the use of machine learning systems in justice sector given the risks to fair trial and litigants' rights.[58]

c) Outline clear lines of accountability for the development and implementation of machine learning systems and clarify which bodies or individuals are legally responsible for decisions made through the use of such systems.

d) Provide effective remedies to victims of discriminatory harms linked to machine learning systems used by public or private bodies, including reparation that, where appropriate, can involve compensation, sanctions against those responsible, and guarantees of non-repetition. This may be possible using existing laws and regulations or may require developing new ones.

Conclusion

57. The signatories of this Declaration call for public and private sector actors to uphold their obligations and responsibilities under human rights laws and standards to avoid discrimination in the use of machine learning systems where possible. Where discrimination arises, measures to deliver the right to effective remedy must be in place.

58. We call on states and private sector actors to work together and play an active and committed role in protecting individuals and groups from discrimination. When creating and deploying machine learning systems, they must take meaningful measures to promote accountability and human rights, including, but not limited to, the right to equality and non-discrimination, as per their obligations and responsibilities under international human rights law and standards.

59. Technological advances must not undermine our human rights. We are at a crossroads where those with the power must act now to protect

---

[58] For example, see: Julia Angwin, Jeff Larson, Surya Mattu and Lauren Kirchner for ProPublica, *Machine Bias*, 2016, https://www.propublica.org/article/machine-bias-risk-assessments-in-criminal-sentencing

human rights, and help safeguard the rights that we are all entitled to now, and for future generations.

UNI Global Union, Top 10 Principles for
Ethical Artificial Intelligence
(2017)

Introduction

As Artificial intelligence (AI), robotics, data and machine learning enter our workplaces across the world displacing and disrupting workers and jobs, unions must get involved. This document provides unions, shop stewards and workers with a set of concrete demands to the transparency, and application of AI. It will inform AI designers and management of the importance of worker inclusion. There is a definite urgency of now. Action is required to safeguard workers' interests and maintain a healthy balance of power in workplaces. The 10 principles provided in this document are developed by UNI Global Union for this purpose.

AI is present in many household appliances and workplaces: in chatbots, robots, system analytics and databases churning out information and reactions such as movements and speech. It has usefully been defined by Arvind Narayanan, Princeton University, as "When behaviour comes not purely from the programmer, but some other means, e.g. knowledge bases."

Data is the building blocks of AI; sometimes simple data algorithms, but increasingly also more complex threads of multiple datasets combined into every longer code.

Artificial intelligence is not a new phenomenon. It has been around for 40 or even 50 years. But the rise of digital technologies, and the vast amount of data produced each day by you and me, has given AI a new significance and a whole new dimension: machine learning. Machine learning is an application of artificial intelligence (AI) that provides systems the ability to automatically learn and improve from experience without being explicitly programmed. Machine learning focuses on the development of computer programs that can access data and use it to learn for themselves.

Hence, we now have forms of added intelligence that can self-learn. In a never-ending spiraling learning process, what started as data derived from all of us, where humans tell the computer that an image portrays a road sign, a cancer cell, a person or car, the machines – based on previous information – can figure that out themselves. They too can find complex correlations between data sets. One such example is that researchers with AI as a tool have now found the seven conditions that need to be in a person's life, for that person later in life to develop a depression.

AI and the World of Work

AI and its applications are already displacing workers, and with the rapid development in its capabilities, it is expected that many more tasks done by humans today, will be done by AI and robots in the future. Within companies, typical human resource tasks are being complemented or even substituted by AI. This can be seen in the use of AI in recruitment and promotion processes, and in workplace monitoring and efficiency/productivity tests. Precisely because of this, unions must be involved in understanding AI, its potentials and challenges to the world of work, and push to have influence over its application.

Some workers are already losing their jobs to AI; indeed, research indicates that over 50% of the work currently done by humans can be faster and more efficiently done by automated systems. AI, machine learning, robotics and automated systems can also benefit workers. In the healthcare sector, robots will be able to help workers lift patients, or monitor their wellbeing. In many service jobs, AI systems can improve the service offered to customers as ever-growing databases of information can support the worker in offering the right service and giving the correct information.

For AI and all its applications to be implemented in a sustainable and ethical way, trade unions must call for insights, influence and rights in relation to the management decisions based fully, or partially, on AI. Across the world only a few company agreements currently exist that include these workers' rights.

Experts agree that now is the time to discuss and determine the appropriate use of AI. UNI Global Union has called for a global convention on ethical AI that will help address, and work to prevent, the unintended negative consequences of AI while accentuating its benefits to workers and society. We underline that humans and corporations are the responsible agents.

This document operationalises UNI Global Union's key demand: Artificial intelligence must put people and planet first. This is why ethical AI discussions on a global scale are essential. A global convention on ethical AI that encompasses all is the most viable guarantee for human survival.

The following offers 10 principles and specific points of action, which unions, shop stewards and global alliances must implement in collective agreements, global framework agreements and multinational alliances. Taking this action will ensure workers' rights and influence in the age of digitalisation.

1. Demand That AI Systems Are Transparent

A transparent artificial intelligence system is one in which it is possible to discover how, and why, the system made a decision, or in the case of a robot, acted the way it did.

In particular:

A. We stress that open source code is neither necessary nor sufficient for transparency – clarity cannot be obfuscated by complexity.

B. For users, transparency is important because it builds trust in, and understanding of, the system, by providing a simple way for the user to understand what the system is doing and why.

C. For validation and certification of an AI system, transparency is important because it exposes the system's processes for scrutiny.

D. If accidents occur, the AI will need to be transparent and accountable to an accident investigator, so the internal process that led to the accident can be understood.

E. Workers must have the right to demand transparency in the decisions and outcomes of AI systems as well as the underlying algorithms (see principle 4 below). This includes the right to appeal decisions made by AI/algorithms, and having it reviewed by a human being.

F. Workers must be consulted on AI systems' implementation, development and deployment.

G. Following an accident, judges, juries, lawyers, and expert witnesses involved in the trial process require transparency and accountability to inform evidence and decision-making.

The principle of transparency is a prerequisite for ascertaining that the remaining principles are observed.

See Principle 2 below for operational solution.

2. Equip AI Systems With an "Ethical Black Box"

Full transparency in an AI system should be facilitated by the presence of a device that can record information about said system in the form of an "ethical black box" that not only contains relevant data to ensure transparency and accountability of a system, but also includes clear data and information on the ethical considerations built into said system.

Applied to robots, the ethical black box would record all decisions, its bases for decision- making, movements, and sensory data for its robot host. The data provided by the black box could also assist robots in explaining their actions in language human users can understand, fostering better relationships and improving the user experience. The read out of the ethical black box should be uncomplicated and fast.

3. Make AI Serve People and Planet

This includes codes of ethics for the development, application and use of AI so that throughout their entire operational process, AI systems remain compatible and increase the principles of human dignity, integrity, freedom, privacy and cultural and gender diversity, as well as with fundamental human rights.

In addition, AI systems must protect and even improve our planet's ecosystems and biodiversity.

4. Adopt a Human-In-Command Approach

An absolute precondition is that the development of AI must be responsible, safe and useful, where machines maintain the legal status of tools, and legal persons retain control over, and responsibility for, these machines *at all times*.

This entails that AI systems should be designed and operated to comply with existing law, including privacy. Workers should have the right to access, manage and control the data AI systems generate, given said systems' power to analyse and utilize that data (See principle 1 in "Top 10 principles for workers' data privacy and protection"). Workers must also have the 'right of explanation' when AI systems are used in human-resource procedures, such as recruitment, promotion or dismissal.

5. Ensure a Genderless, Unbiased AI

In the design and maintenance of AI, it is vital that the system is controlled for negative or harmful human-bias, and that any bias—be it gender, race, sexual orientation, age, etc.—is identified and is not propagated by the system.

6. Share the Benefits of AI Systems

AI technologies should benefit and empower as many people as possible. The economic

prosperity created by AI should be distributed broadly and equally, to benefit all of humanity.

Global as well as national policies aimed at bridging the economic, technological and social digital divide are therefore necessary.

7. Secure a Just Transition and Ensuring Support for Fundamental Freedoms and Rights

As AI systems develop and augmented realities are formed, workers and work tasks will be displaced. To ensure a just transition, as well as sustainable future developments, it is vital that corporate policies are put in place that ensure corporate accountability in relation to this displacement, such as retraining programmes and job change possibilities. Governmental measures to help displaced workers retrain and find new employment are additionally required.

AI systems coupled with the wider transition to the digital economy will require that workers on all levels and in all occupations have access to social security and to continuous lifelong learning to remain employable. It is the responsibility of states and companies to find solutions that provide all workers, in all forms of work, the right to and access to both.

In addition, in a world where the casualisation or individualisation of work is rising, all workers in all forms of work must have the same, strong social and fundamental rights. All AI systems must include a check and balance on whether its deployment and augmentation go hand in hand with workers' rights as laid out in human right laws, ILO conventions and collective agreements. An algorithm "8798" reflecting the core ILO conventions 87 and 98 that is built into the system could serve that very purpose. Upon failure, the system must be shut down.

8. Establish Global Governance Mechanisms

UNI recommends the establishment of multi-stakeholder Decent Work and Ethical AI governance bodies on global and regional levels. The bodies should include AI designers, manufacturers, owners, developers, researchers, employers, lawyers, CSOs and trade unions. Whistleblowing mechanisms and monitoring procedures to ensure the transition to, and implementation of, ethical AI must be established. The bodies should be granted the competence to recommend compliance processes and procedures.

9. Ban the Attribution of Responsibility to Robots

Robots should be designed and operated as far as is practicable to comply with existing laws, fundamental rights and freedoms, including privacy. This is linked to the question of *legal responsibility*. In line with Bryson et al 2011, UNI Global Union asserts that legal responsibility for a robot should be attributed to a person. Robots are not responsible parties under the law.

10. Ban AI Arms Race

Lethal autonomous weapons, including cyber warfare, should be banned.

FAT/ML, Principles for Accountable Algorithms and a Social Impact Statement for Algorithms (2016)

Principles for Accountable Algorithms

Automated decision making algorithms are now used throughout industry and government, underpinning many processes from dynamic pricing to employment practices to criminal sentencing. Given that such algorithmically informed decisions have the potential for significant societal impact, the goal of this document is to help developers and product managers design and implement algorithmic systems in publicly accountable ways. Accountability in this context includes an obligation to report, explain, or justify algorithmic decision-making as well as mitigate any negative social impacts or potential harms.

We begin by outlining five equally important guiding principles that follow from this premise:

Algorithms and the data that drive them are designed and created by people -- There is always a human ultimately responsible for decisions made or informed by an algorithm. "The algorithm did it" is not an acceptable excuse if algorithmic systems make mistakes or have undesired consequences, including from machine-learning processes.

Responsibility

Make available externally visible avenues of redress for adverse individual or societal effects of an algorithmic decision system, and designate an internal role for the person who is responsible for the timely remedy of such issues.

Explainability

Ensure that algorithmic decisions as well as any data driving those decisions can be explained to end-users and other stakeholders in non-technical terms.

Accuracy

Identify, log, and articulate sources of error and uncertainty throughout the algorithm and its data sources so that expected and worst case implications can be understood and inform mitigation procedures.

Auditability

Enable interested third parties to probe, understand, and review the behavior of the algorithm through disclosure of information that enables monitoring, checking, or criticism, including through provision of detailed documentation, technically suitable APIs, and permissive terms of use.

Fairness

Ensure that algorithmic decisions do not create discriminatory or unjust impacts when comparing across different demographics (e.g. race, sex, etc).

We have left some of the terms above purposefully under-specified to allow these principles to be broadly applicable. Applying these principles well should include understanding them within a specific context. We also suggest that these issues be revisited and discussed throughout the design, implementation, and release phases of development. Two important principles for consideration were purposefully left off of this list as they are well-covered elsewhere: privacy and the impact of human experimentation. We encourage you to incorporate those issues into your overall assessment of algorithmic accountability as well.

Social Impact Statement for Algorithms

In order to ensure their adherence to these principles and to publicly commit to associated best practices, we propose that algorithm creators develop a Social Impact Statement using the above principles as a guiding structure. This statement should be revisited and reassessed (at least) three times during the design and development process:

- design stage,

- pre-launch,

- and post-launch.

When the system is launched, the statement should be made public as a form of transparency so that the public has expectations for social impact of the system.

The Social Impact Statement should minimally answer the questions below. Included below are concrete steps that can be taken, and documented as part of the statement, to address these questions. These questions and steps make up an outline of such a social impact statement.

Responsibility

Guiding Questions

- Who is responsible if users are harmed by this product?

- What will the reporting process and process for recourse be?

- Who will have the power to decide on necessary changes to the algorithmic system during design stage, pre-launch, and post-launch?

Initial Steps to Take

- Determine and designate a person who will be responsible for the social impact of the algorithm.

- Make contact information available so that if there are issues it's clear to users how to proceed

- Develop a plan for what to do if the project has unintended consequences. This may be part of a maintenance plan and should involve post-launch monitoring plans.

- Develop a sunset plan for the system to manage algorithm or data risks after the product is no longer in active development.

Explainability

Guiding Questions

- Who are your end-users and stakeholders?

- How much of your system / algorithm can you explain to your users and stakeholders?

- How much of the data sources can you disclose?

Initial Steps to Take

- Have a plan for how decisions will be explained to users and subjects of those decisions. In some cases it may be appropriate to develop an automated explanation for each decision.

- Allow data subjects visibility into the data you store about them and access to a process in order to change it.

- If you are using a machine-learning model:

    o consider whether a directly interpretable or explainable model can be used.

    o describe the training data including how, when, and why it was collected and sampled.

    o describe how and when test data about an individual that is used to make a decision is collected or inferred.

- Disclose the sources of any data used and as much as possible about the specific attributes of the data. Explain how the data was cleaned or otherwise transformed.

<u>**Accuracy**</u>

Guiding Questions

- What sources of error do you have and how will you mitigate their effect?

- How confident are the decisions output by your algorithmic system?

- What are realistic worst case scenarios in terms of how errors might impact society, individuals, and stakeholders?

- Have you evaluated the provenance and veracity of data and considered alternative data sources?

Initial Steps to Take

- Assess the potential for errors in your system and the resulting potential for harm to users.

- Undertake a sensitivity analysis to assess how uncertainty in the output of the algorithm relates to uncertainty in the inputs.

- Develop a process by which people can correct errors in input data, training data, or in output decisions.

- Perform a validity check by randomly sampling a portion of your data (e.g., input and/or training data) and manually checking its correctness. This check should be performed early in your development process before derived information is used. Report the overall data error rate on this random sample publicly.

- Determine how to communicate the uncertainty / margin of error for each decision.

<u>Auditability</u>

Guiding Questions

- Can you provide for public auditing (i.e. probing, understanding, reviewing of system behavior) or is there sensitive information that would necessitate auditing by a designated 3rd party?

- How will you facilitate public or third-party auditing without opening the system to unwarranted manipulation?

Initial Steps to Take

- Document and make available an API that allows third parties to query the algorithmic system and assess its response.

- Make sure that if data is needed to properly audit your algorithm, such as in the case of a machine-learning algorithm, that sample (e.g., training) data is made available.

- Make sure your terms of service allow the research community to perform automated public audits.

- Have a plan for communication with outside parties that may be interested in auditing your algorithm, such as the research and development community.

Fairness

Guiding Questions

- Are there particular groups which may be advantaged or disadvantaged, in the context in which you are deploying, by the algorithm / system you are building?

- What is the potential damaging effect of uncertainty / errors to different groups?

Initial Steps to Take

- Talk to people who are familiar with the subtle social context in which you are deploying. For example, you should consider whether the following aspects of people's identities will have impacts on their equitable access to and results from your system:

- Race

- Sex

- Gender identity

- Ability status

- Socio-economic status

- Education level

- Religion

- Country of origin

- If you are building an automated decision-making tool, you should deploy a fairness-aware data mining algorithm. (See, e.g., the resources gathered at http://fatml.org).

- Calculate the error rates and types (e.g., false positives vs. false negatives) for different sub-populations and assess the potential differential impacts.

Corporate AI Guidelines

IBM, Everyday Ethics for Artificial Intelligence (2018)
(footnotes note included)

Accountability

AI designers and developers are responsible for considering AI design, development, decision processes, and outcomes. Accountability

Human judgment plays a role throughout a seemingly objective system of logical decisions. It is humans who write algorithms, who define success or failure, who make decisions about the uses of systems and who may be affected by a system's outcomes. Every person involved in the creation of AI at any step is accountable for considering the system's impact in the world, as are the companies invested in its development.

Recommended actions to take

01 Make company policies clear and accessible to design and development teams from day one so that no one is confused about issues of responsibility or accountability. As an AI designer or developer, it is your responsibility to know.

02 Understand where the responsibility of the company/software ends. You may not have control over how data or a tool will be used by a user, client, or other external source.

03 Keep detailed records of your design processes and decision making. Determine a strategy for keeping records during the design and development process to encourage best practices [*sic*].

04 Adhere to your company's business conduct guidelines. Also, understand national and international laws, regulations, and guidelines that your AI may have to work within. You can find other related resources in the IEEE Ethically Aligned Design document.

...

Value Alignment

AI should be designed to align with the norms and values of your user group in mind.

AI works alongside diverse, human interests. People make decisions based on any number of contextual factors, including their experiences, memories, upbringing, and cultural norms. These factors allow us to have a fundamental understanding of "right and wrong" in a wide range of contexts, at home, in the office, or elsewhere. This is second nature for humans, as we have a wealth of experiences to draw upon. Today's AI systems do not have these types of experiences to draw upon, so it is the job of designers and developers to collaborate with each other in order to ensure consideration of existing values. Care is required to ensure sensitivity to a wide range of cultural norms and values. As daunting as it may seem to take value systems into account, the common core of universal principles is that they are a cooperative phenomenon. Successful teams already understand that cooperation and collaboration leads to the best outcomes.

Recommended actions to take

01 Consider the culture that establishes the value systems you're designing within. Whenever possible, bring in policymakers and academics that can help your team articulate relevant perspectives.

02 Work with design researchers to understand and reflect your users' values. You can find out more about this process here.

03 Consider mapping out your understanding of your users' values and aligning the AI's actions accordingly with an Ethics Canvas. Values will be specific to certain use cases and affected communities. Alignment will allow users to better understand your AI's actions and intents.

. . .

Explainability

AI should be designed for humans to easily perceive, detect, and understand its decision process.

In general, we don't blindly trust those who can't explain their reasoning. The same goes for AI, perhaps even more so. As an AI increases in capabilities and achieves a greater range of impact, its decision-making process should be explainable in terms people can understand.

Explainability is key for users interacting with AI to understand the AI's conclusions and recommendations. Your users should always be aware that they are interacting with an AI. Good design does not sacrifice transparency in creating a seamless experience. Imperceptible AI is not ethical AI.

Recommended actions to take

01 Allow for questions. A user should be able to ask why an AI is doing what it's doing on an ongoing basis. This should be clear and up front in the user interface at all times.

02 Decision making processes must be reviewable, especially if the AI is working with highly sensitive personal information data like personally identifiable information, protected health information, and/or biometric data.

03 When an AI is assisting users with making any highly sensitive decisions, the AI must be able to provide them with a sufficient explanation of recommendations, the data used, and the reasoning behind the recommendations.

04 Teams should have and maintain access to a record of an AI's decision processes and be amenable to verification of those decision processes.

. . .

Fairness

AI must be designed to minimize bias and promote inclusive representation.

AI provides deeper insight into our personal lives when interacting with our sensitive data. As humans are inherently vulnerable to biases, and are responsible for building AI, there are chances for human bias to be embedded in the systems we create. It is the role of a responsible team to minimize algorithmic bias through ongoing research and data collection which is representative of a diverse population.

Recommended actions to take

01 Real-time analysis of AI brings to light both intentional and unintentional biases. When bias in data becomes apparent, the team must investigate and understand where it originated and how it can be mitigated.

02 Design and develop without intentional biases and schedule team reviews to avoid unintentional biases. Unintentional biases can include stereotyping, confirmation bias, and sunk cost bias....

03 Instill a feedback mechanism or open dialogue with users to raise awareness of user-identified biases or issues. e.g., Woebot asks "Let me know what you think," after suggesting a link

. . .

User Data Rights

AI must be designed to protect user data and preserve the user's power over access and uses.

It is your team's responsibility to keep users empowered with control over their interactions.

Pew Research recently found that being in control of our own information is "very important" to 74% of Americans. The European Commission found that 71% of EU citizens find it unacceptable for companies to share information about them without their permission. These percentages will rise as AI is further used to either amplify our privacy or undermine it. Your company should be fully compliant with the applicable portions of EU's General Data Protection Regulation and any comparable regulations in other countries, to make sure users understand that AI is working in their best interests.

Recommended actions to take

01 Users should always maintain control over what data is being used and in what context. They can deny access to personal data that they may find compromising or unfit for an AI to know or use.

02 Users' data should be protected from theft, misuse, or data corruption.

03 Provide full disclosure on how the personal information is being used or shared.

04 Allow users to deny service or data by having the AI ask for permission before an interaction or providing the option during an interaction. Privacy settings and permissions should be clear, findable, and adjustable.

05 Forbid use of another company's data without permission when creating a new AI service.

06 Recognize and adhere to applicable national and international rights laws when designing for an AI's acceptable user data access permissions.

...

Google CEO Sundar Pichai,
AI at Google: Our Principles
(2018)

At its heart, AI is computer programming that learns and adapts. It can't solve every problem, but its potential to improve our lives is profound. At Google, we use AI to make products more useful—from email that's spam-free and easier to compose, to a digital assistant you can speak to naturally, to photos that pop the fun stuff out for you to enjoy.

Beyond our products, we're using AI to help people tackle urgent problems. A pair of high school students are building AI-powered sensors to predict the risk of wildfires. Farmers are using it to monitor the health of their herds. Doctors are starting to use AI to help diagnose cancer and prevent blindness. These clear benefits are why Google invests heavily in AI research and development, and makes AI technologies widely available to others via our tools and open-source code.

We recognize that such powerful technology raises equally powerful questions about its use. How AI is developed and used will have a significant impact on society for many years to come. As a leader in AI, we feel a deep responsibility to get this right. So today, we're announcing seven principles to guide our work going forward. These are not theoretical concepts; they are concrete standards that will actively govern our research and product development and will impact our business decisions.

We acknowledge that this area is dynamic and evolving, and we will approach our work with humility, a commitment to internal and external engagement, and a willingness to adapt our approach as we learn over time.

Objectives for AI applications

We will assess AI applications in view of the following objectives. We believe that AI should:

1. Be socially beneficial.

The expanded reach of new technologies increasingly touches society as a whole. Advances in AI will have transformative impacts in a wide range of fields, including healthcare, security, energy, transportation, manufacturing, and entertainment. As we consider potential development and uses of AI technologies, we will take into account a broad range of social and economic factors, and will proceed where we believe that the overall likely benefits substantially exceed the foreseeable risks and downsides.

AI also enhances our ability to understand the meaning of content at scale. We will strive to make high-quality and accurate information readily available using AI, while continuing to respect cultural, social, and legal norms in the countries where we operate. And we will continue to thoughtfully evaluate when to make our technologies available on a non-commercial basis.

2. Avoid creating or reinforcing unfair bias.

AI algorithms and datasets can reflect, reinforce, or reduce unfair biases. We recognize that distinguishing fair from unfair biases is not always simple, and differs across cultures and societies. We will seek to avoid unjust impacts on people, particularly those related to sensitive characteristics such as race, ethnicity, gender, nationality, income, sexual orientation, ability, and political or religious belief.

3. Be built and tested for safety.

We will continue to develop and apply strong safety and security practices to avoid unintended results that create risks of harm. We will design our AI systems to be appropriately cautious, and seek to develop them in accordance with best practices in AI safety research. In appropriate cases, we will test AI technologies in constrained environments and monitor their operation after deployment.

4. Be accountable to people.

We will design AI systems that provide appropriate opportunities for feedback, relevant explanations, and appeal. Our AI technologies will be subject to appropriate human direction and control.

5. Incorporate privacy design principles.

We will incorporate our privacy principles in the development and use of our AI technologies. We will give opportunity for notice and consent, encourage architectures with privacy safeguards, and provide appropriate transparency and control over the use of data.

6. Uphold high standards of scientific excellence.

Technological innovation is rooted in the scientific method and a commitment to open inquiry, intellectual rigor, integrity, and collaboration. AI tools have the potential to unlock new realms of scientific research and knowledge in critical domains like biology, chemistry, medicine, and environmental sciences. We aspire to high standards of scientific excellence as we work to progress AI development.

We will work with a range of stakeholders to promote thoughtful leadership in this area, drawing on scientifically rigorous and multidisciplinary approaches. And we will responsibly share AI knowledge by publishing educational materials, best practices, and research that enable more people to develop useful AI applications.

7. Be made available for uses that accord with these principles.

Many technologies have multiple uses. We will work to limit potentially harmful or abusive applications. As we develop and deploy AI technologies, we will evaluate likely uses in light of the following factors:

- *Primary purpose and use:* the primary purpose and likely use of a technology and application, including how closely the solution is related to or adaptable to a harmful use

- *Nature and uniqueness:* whether we are making available technology that is unique or more generally available

- *Scale:* whether the use of this technology will have significant impact

- *Nature of Google's involvement:* whether we are providing general-purpose tools, integrating tools for customers, or developing custom solutions

AI applications we will not pursue

In addition to the above objectives, we will not design or deploy AI in the following application areas:

1. Technologies that cause or are likely to cause overall harm. Where there is a material risk of harm, we will proceed only where we believe that the benefits substantially outweigh the risks, and will incorporate appropriate safety constraints.

2. Weapons or other technologies whose principal purpose or implementation is to cause or directly facilitate injury to people.

3. Technologies that gather or use information for surveillance violating internationally accepted norms.

4. Technologies whose purpose contravenes widely accepted principles of international law and human rights.

We want to be clear that while we are not developing AI for use in weapons, we will continue our work with governments and the military in many other areas. These include cybersecurity, training, military recruitment, veterans' healthcare, and search and rescue. These collaborations are important and we'll actively look for more ways to augment the critical work of these organizations and keep service members and civilians safe.

AI for the long term

While this is how we're choosing to approach AI, we understand there is room for many voices in this conversation. As AI technologies progress, we'll work with a range of stakeholders to promote thoughtful leadership in this area, drawing on scientifically rigorous and multidisciplinary approaches. And we will continue to share what we've learned to improve AI technologies and practices.

We believe these principles are the right foundation for our company and the future development of AI. This approach is consistent with the values laid out in our original Founders' Letter back in 2004. There we made clear our intention to take a long-term perspective, even if it means making short-term tradeoffs. We said it then, and we believe it now.

Microsoft, AI Principles
(2018)

Designing AI to be trustworthy requires creating solutions that reflect ethical principles that are deeply rooted in important and timeless values.

Fairness

AI systems should treat all people fairly

Inclusiveness

AI systems should empower everyone and engage people

Reliability & Safety

AI systems should perform reliably and safely

Transparency

AI systems should be understandable

Privacy & Security

AI systems should be secure and respect privacy

Accountability

AI systems should have algorithmic accountability

Telefonica,
Our Artificial Intelligence Principles
(2018)

Big Data and Artificial Intelligence (AI) allow us to transform business, people's lives and society. With these advances, we want to improve as a company at the same time as making the world a better place for everyone. To do so, we are committed to designing, developing, and using an AI that is:

Fair

We ensure that applications do not lead to biased results and unfair and discriminatory impacts. We guarantee that there are no discriminatory elements when AI learns and algorithms decide.

Transparent and Explainable

We inform users of the data that we use and its purpose. We take sufficient measures to ensure the understanding of the AI's decisions. We tell our users when they are interacting with an AI system.

Human0Centric

We ensure that AI always respects human rights. We are committed to the UN Sustainable Development Goals. We contribute to preventing improper use of technology.

Privacy and Security by Design

To build Artificial Intelligence systems, we take special care of information security. We respect the right to privacy of people and their data.

With Partners and Third Parties

We confirm the veracity of the logic and the data used by the suppliers.

Sony Group,
AI Ethics Guidelines
(2018)

Scope of the Guidelines

The "Sony Group AI Ethics Guidelines" (Guidelines) set forth the guidelines that must be followed by all officers and employees of Sony when utilizing AI and/or conducting AI-related R&D.

"Utilization of AI" within Sony means the following:

1. The provision of products and services by Sony, including entertainment content and financial services, which utilize AI; and

2. The usage of AI for various purposes by Sony in its business activities such as R&D, product manufacturing, service provision, and other operational activities.

Definitions in the Guidelines

"AI" means any functionality or its enabling technology that performs information processing for various purposes that people perceive as intelligent, and that is embodied by machine learning based on data, or by rules or knowledge extracted in some methods.

"Sony" means Sony Corporation and any company where more than 50% of voting rights are directly or indirectly owned by Sony Corporation.

Revision of the Guidelines

Sony will review and evolve the Guidelines as needed based on national and regional AI-related guidelines, changes in people's lifestyles and environments, accumulation of practices in the relevant industry, and information exchanged with its various stakeholders.

1. Supporting Creative Life Styles and Building a Better Society

Through advancing its AI-related R&D and promoting the utilization of AI in a manner harmonized with society, Sony aims to support the exploration of the potential for each individual to empower their lives, and to contribute to enrichment of our culture and push our civilization forward by providing novel and creative types of kando. Sony will engage in sustainable social development and endeavor to utilize the power of AI for contributing to global problem-solving and for the development of a peaceful and sustainable society.

2. Stakeholder Engagement

In order to solve the challenges arising from use of AI while striving for better AI utilization, Sony will seriously consider the interests and concerns of various stakeholders including its customers and creators, and proactively advance a dialogue with related industries, organizations, academic communities and more. For this purpose, Sony will construct the appropriate channels for ensuring that the content and results of these discussions are provided to officers and employees, including researchers and developers, who are involved in the corresponding businesses, as well as for ensuring further engagement with its various stakeholders.

3. Provision of Trusted Products and Services

Sony understands the need for safety when dealing with products and services utilizing AI and will continue to respond to security risks such as unauthorized access. AI systems may utilize statistical or probabilistic methods to achieve results. In the interest of Sony's customers and to maintain their trust, Sony will design whole systems with an awareness of the responsibility associated with the characteristics of such methods.

4. Privacy Protection

Sony, in compliance with laws and regulations as well as applicable internal rules and policies, seeks to enhance the security and protection of customers' personal data acquired via products and services utilizing AI, and build an environment where said personal data is processed in ways that respect the intention and trust of customers.

5. Respect for Fairness

In its utilization of AI, Sony will respect diversity and human rights of its customers and other stakeholders without any discrimination while striving to contribute to the resolution of social problems through its activities in its own and related industries.

6. Pursuit of Transparency

During the planning and design stages for its products and services that utilize AI, Sony will strive to introduce methods of capturing the reasoning behind the decisions made by AI utilized in said products and services. Additionally, it will endeavor to provide intelligible explanations and information to customers about the possible impact of using these products and services.

7. The Evolution of AI and Ongoing Education

People's lives have continuously changed with the advance in technology across history. Sony will be cognizant of the effects and impact of products and services that utilize AI on society and will proactively work to contribute to developing AI to create a better society and foster human talent capable of shaping our collective bright future through R&D and/or utilization of AI.

Deutsche Telekom,
AI Guidelines
(2018)

Preamble

Two of Deutsche Telekom's most important goals are to keep being a trusted companion and to enhance customer experience.

We see it as our responsibility - as one of the leading ICT companies in Europe - to foster the development of "intelligent technologies". At least either important, these technologies, such as AI, must follow predefined ethical rules.

To define a corresponding ethical framework, firstly it needs a common understanding on what AI means. Today there are several definitions of AI, like the very first one of John McCarthy (1956) "Every aspect of learning or any other feature of intelligence can in principle be so precisely described that a machine can be made to simulate it." In line with other companies and main players in the field of AI we at DT think of AI as the imitation of human intelligence processes by machines, especially computer systems. These processes include learning, reasoning, and self-correction.

After several decades, Artificial Intelligence has become one of the most intriguing topics of today – and the future. It has become widespread available and is discussed not only among experts but also more and more in public, politics, etc.. AI has started to influence business (new market opportunities as well as efficiency driver), society (e.g. broad discussion about autonomously driving vehicles or AI as "job machine" vs. "job killer") and the life of each individual (AI already found its way into the living room, e.g. with voice steered digital assistants like smart speakers).

But the use of AI and its possibilities confront us not only with fast developing technologies but as well as with the fact that our ethical roadmaps, based on human-human interactions, might not be sufficient in this new era of technological influence. New questions arise and situations that were not imaginable in our daily lives then emerge.

We as DT also want to develop and make use of AI. This technology can bring many benefits based on improving customer experience or simplicity. We are already in the game, e.g having several AI-related projects running. With these comes an increase of digital responsibility on our side to ensure that AI is utilized in an ethical manner. So we as DT have to give answers to our customers, shareholders and stakeholders.

The following Digital Ethics guidelines state how we as Deutsche Telekom want to build the future with AI. For us, technology serves one main purpose: It must act supportingly. Thus AI is in any case supposed to extend and complement human abilities rather than lessen them.

Remark: The impact of AI on DT jobs – may it as a benefit and for value creation in the sense of job enrichment and enlargement or may it in the sense of efficiency - is however not focus of these guidelines.

1. We are responsible. The human always remains responsible. Our solutions come with a clear definition of who is responsible for which AI system or feature. We are in charge of our products and services. And, we know who is in charge for partner or third party solutions.

With AI technology being in its infancy, we are aware of our responsibility in development – from the very beginning. We make sure that we clarify which initiative or product owner has which responsibilities. For partners or third parties, we define clear guidelines for when a partnership can be established. And, we declare which duties are connected to the respective AI parts.

2. We care. We act in tune with our company values. Our systems and solutions must subordinate to humandefined rules and laws. Therefore, in addition to our technical requirements, our systems and solutions have to obey the rules and laws that we as Deutsche Telekom, our employees – and human beings as such – follow.

AI systems have to meet the same high technical requirements as any other IT system of ours, such as security, robustness, etc. But since AI will be (and already is) a great part of our everyday lives, even guiding us in several areas, AI systems and their usage also have to comply with our company values (Deutsche Telekom's Guiding Principles and Code of Conduct), ethical values, and societal conventions. We have to make sure of that.

3. We put our customers first. We enrich and simplify our customers' lives. If an AI system or the usage of customer-related data helps us to benefit our customers, we embrace this opportunity to meet their demands and expectations.

The aggregation and use of customer data – especially in AI systems – shall always be clear and serve a useful purpose towards our customers. Systems and processes that support in the background are as important as services that interact with our customers directly.

4. We are transparent. In no case we hide it when the customer's counterpart is an AI. And, we are transparent about how we use customer data. As Deutsche Telekom, we always have the customer's trust in mind – trust is what we stand for.

We are acting openly to our customers. It is obvious to our customers that they are interacting with an AI when they do. In addition, we make clear, how and to which extent they can choose the way of further processing their personal data.

5. We are secure. Data security is a prime quality of Deutsche Telekom. In order to maintain this asset, we ensure that our security measures are up to date while having a full overview of how customer related data is used and who has access to which kind of data.

We never process privacy-relevant data without legal permission. This policy applies to our AI systems just as much as it does to all of our activities. Additionally, we limit the usage to appropriate use cases and thoroughly secure our systems to obstruct external access and ensure data privacy

6. We set the framework. Our AI solutions are developed and enhanced on grounds of deep analysis and evaluation. They are transparent, auditable, fair, and fully documented. We consciously initiate the AI's development for the best possible outcome.

The essential paradigm for our AI systems' impact analysis is "privacy und security by design". This is accompanied e.g. by risks and chances scenarios or reliable disaster scenarios. We take great care in the initial algorithm of our own AI solutions to prevent so called "Black Boxes" and to make sure that our systems shall not unintentionally harm the users.

7. We maintain control. We are able to deactivate and stop AI systems at any time (kill switch). Additionally, we remove inappropriate data to avoid bias. We have an eye on the decisions made and the information fed to the system in order to enhance decision quality.

We take responsibility for a diverse and appropriate data input. In case of inconsistencies, we rather stop the AI system than pursue with potentially manipulated data. We are also able to "reset" our AI systems in order to remove false or biased data. By this, we install a lever to reduce (unintended) unsuitable decisions or actions to a minimum.

8. We foster the cooperative model. We believe that human and machine intelligence are complementary, with each bringing its own strength to the table. While we believe in a people first approach of human-machine collaboration, we recognize, that humans can benefit from the strength of AI to unfold a potential that neither human or machine can unlock on its own.

We recognize the widespread fear, that AI enabled machines will outsmart the human intelligence. We as Deutsche Telekom think differently. We know and believe in the human strengths like inspiration, intuition, sense making and empathy. But we also recognize the strengths of AI like data recall, processing speed and analysis. By combining both, AI systems will help humans to make better decisions and accomplish objectives more effective and efficient.

9. We share and enlighten. We acknowledge the transformative power of AI for our society. We will support people and society in preparing for this future world. We live our digital responsibility by sharing our knowledge, pointing out the opportunities of the new technology without neglecting its risks. We will engage with our customers, other companies, policy makers, education institutions and all other stakeholders to ensure we understand their concerns and needs and can setup the right safeguards. We will engage in AI and ethics education. Hereby preparing ourselves, our colleagues and our fellow human beings for the new tasks ahead.

Many tasks that are being executed by humans now will be automated in the future. This leads to a shift in the demand of skills. Jobs will be reshaped, rather replaced by AI. While this seems certain, the minority knows what exactly AI technology is capable of achieving. Prejudice and sciolism lead to either demonization of progress or to blind acknowledgment, both calling for educational work. We as Deutsche Telekom feel responsible to enlighten people and help society to deal with the digital shift, so that new appropriate skills can be developed and new jobs can be taken over. And we start from within – by enabling our colleagues and employees. But we are aware that this task cannot be solved by one company alone. Therefore we will engage in partnerships with other companies, offer our know-how to policy makers and education providers to jointly tackle the challenges ahead.

AI Resources

Organizations

Access Now
P.O. Box 20429
Greeley Square Station
4 East 27th Street
New York, NY 10001-9998
1-888-414-0100
info@accessnow.org
https://privacyinternational.org/topics/artificial-intelligence

Artículo 12
Mexico
http://articulo12.org/

AI4ALL
Oakland, CA
http://ai-4-all.org

AI Ethics Lab
Boston, Massachusetts, Turkey
contact@aiethicslab.com
http://aiethicslab.com

AI Now Institute
New York University
New York, NY 10003
info@ainowinstitute.org
https://ainowinstitute.org/

AI World Society
Beacon Hill
Boston, MA 02108
1-617-286-6589

office@bostonglobalforum.org
https://bostonglobalforum.org/category/
publications/ai-world-society/

Algorithmic Justice League
https://www.ajlunited.org

American Association for the Advancement of Science
1200 New York Ave, NW
Washington, DC
20005
1-202-326-6400
https://www.sciencemag.org/topic/artificial-intelligence

American Civil Liberties Union
125 Broad Street, 18th Floor
New York NY 10004
212-549-2500
https://www.aclu.org/issues/privacy-technology

Association for Computing Machinery
1601 Broadway, 10th Floor
New York, NY 10019-7434
1-212-869-7440
https://www.acm.org/

Asociación por los Derechos Civiles
Tucumán 924 8 ° (C1049AAT)
Autonomous City of Buenos
Aires, Buenos Aires
Argentina
54-11-5236-0555
adc@adc.org.ar
https://adc.org.ar/2019/07/18/un
a-perspectiva-de-derechos-para-
el-plan-nacional-de-inteligencia-
artificial/

BEUC, The European Consumer Organisation
Rue d'Arlon, 80 Bte 1
B - 1040 Bruxelles
Belgium
32-2-743-15-90
aja@beuc.eu
https://www.beuc.eu/general/arti
ficial-intelligence

Boston Global Forum
Beacon Hill
Boston, MA 02108
1-617-286-6589
office@bostonglobalforum.org
https://bostonglobalforum.org/ca
tegory/aiws/

The Brookings Institution
1775 Massachusetts Ave., NW
Washington, DC 20036
1-202-797-6000
communications@brookings.edu
https://www.brookings.edu/proje
ct/artificial-intelligence-and-
emerging-technologies-
initiative/

Center for Democracy and Technology
1401 K Street NW, Suite 200
Washington, DC 20005
1-202-637-9800
Hello@cdt.org
https://cdt.org/issue/privacy-
data/digital-decisions/

Center for a New American Security
1152 15th Street, NW
Suite 950
Washington, DC 20005
1-202-457-9400
info@cnas.org
https://www.cnas.org/artificial-
intelligence-and-global-security

Center for Research, Information, Technology and Advanced Computing (CRITAC)
Cape Coast
Ghana
233-20-269-8355
http://critacghana.com/critac/

Colegio Profesional de Ingenieros Técnicos en Informática de Andalucía
PO Box No. 56 - 04080
Almería
Spain
950-70-00-45
https://www.cpitia.org/formulari
o-de-contacto/

Derechos Digitales
Diagonal Paraguay 458
Second floor
8330051 Santiago
Chile
56-2-2702-7108
https://www.derechosdigitales.or
g/11341/cuando-la-tecnologia-
nos-amenaza/

Digital Asia Hub
Hong Kong
dlewis@digitalasiahub.org
https://www.digitalasiahub.org/c
ategory/events/ai-in-asia/

**Electronic Privacy
Information Center**
1519 New Hampshire Avenue
NW
Washington, DC 20036
1-202-483-1140
info@epic.org
https://epic.org/algorithmic-
transparency/

**Fundación Ciudadano
Inteligente**
Chile
https://ciudadaniai.org/

Fundación Vía Libre
Argentina
info@vialibre.org.ar
https://www.vialibre.org.ar/categ
ory/ia

**Foundation for Responsible
Robotics**

Laan van Meerdervoort 70
2517 AN, The Hague
Netherlands
https://responsiblerobotics.org

FullAI
Amsterdam
Netherlands
postbox@fullai.org
http://www.fullai.org/

**Future of Humanity Institute,
Oxford**
Littlegate House, 16-17 St
Ebbe's Street,
Oxford, OX1 1PT
UK
-44-0-1865-286800
fhiea@philosophy.ox.ac.uk
https://www.fhi.ox.ac.uk/contac/

Future of Life Institute
Boston, MA
https://futureoflife.org/ai-news/

The Future Society
Cambridge, MA
https://thefuturesociety.org/conta
ct/

Homo Digitalis
Paralou 12
118 54, Athens-Rouf, Attica
Greece
info@homodigitalis.gr
https://www.homodigitalis.gr/

**Human Rights Data
Analysis Group**
San Francisco, CA
info@hrdag.org
https://hrdag.org/

Human Rights Watch
350 Fifth Ave 34th Floor
New York, NY 10118-3299
1-212-290-4700
https://www.hrw.org/

Ipandetec
Spaces Panama - Plaza 2000
Panama City
Panama
ipandetec@gmail.com
http://www.ipandetec.org/tag/int
eligencia-artificial/

**Institute of Electrical and
Electronics Engineers**
3 Park Avenue, 17th Floor
New York, NY 10016-5997
1-800-678-4333
contactcenter@ieee.org
https://www.ieee.org/

**Instituto Italiano Per La
Privacy E La Valorizzazione
Dei Dati**
Piazza di San Salvatore in Lauro
13 - 00186 - Rome
Italy
39-391-361-42-93
info@istitutoprivacy.it
https://www.istitutoitalianopriva
cy.it/

**Instituto Per Le Politiche
Dell'innovazione**
Via dei Barbieri
6 00186, Rome
Italy
info@istitutoinnovazione.eu
https://istitutoinnovazione.eu/

KICTAnet
Kenya
https://www.kictanet.or.ke/

**Machine Intelligence Research
Institute**
Berkeley, CA
https://intelligence.org/

MIT Media Lab
77 Mass. Ave., E14/E15
Cambridge, MA 02139-4307
web-general@media.mit.edu
https://www.media.mit.edu/grou
ps/ml-learning/overview/

Open AI
San Francisco, California
info@openai.com
https://openai.com

Panoptykon Foundation
ul. Orzechowska 4/4
02-068 Warsaw
Poland
48-660-074-026
fundacja@panoptykon.org
https://panoptykon.org/

Paradigm Initiative
2nd Floor, 385 Herbert
Macaulay Way, Yaba
Lagos, Nigeria
234-1-342-62-45
hello@paradigmhq.org
http://paradigmhq.org/

Partnership on AI
215 2nd St, Ste 200
San Francisco, CA 94105
https://www.partnershiponai.org/

Privacy International
62 Britton Street,
London, EC1M 5UY
UK
https://privacyinternational.org/t
opics/artificial-intelligence

**Schwarzman College of
Computing, MIT**
77 Massachusetts Avenue
Cambridge, MA
http://computing.mit.edu/about/

World Privacy Forum
3 Monroe Pkwy, Suite P #148
Lake Oswego, OR 97035
1-760-712-4281
info@worldprivacyforum.org
https://www.worldprivacyforum.
org/

AI Reports

Access Now, *Human Rights in
the Age of Artificial Intelligence*
(2018),

https://www.accessnow.org/cms/
assets/uploads/2018/11/AI-and-
Human-Rights.pdf

Agency for Digital Italy,
*Artificial Intelligence at the
service of the citizen* (2018),
https://libro-bianco-
ia.readthedocs.io/en/latest/

AI Now Institute, *Litigating
Algorithms: Challenging
Government Use of Algorithmic
Decision Systems* (2018),
https://ainowinstitute.org/litigati
ngalgorithms.pdf

Greg Allen & Taniel Chan,
Harvard Kennedy Belfer Center
*Artificial Intelligence and
National Security* (2017),
https://www.belfercenter.org/site
s/default/files/files/publication/A
I%20NatSec%20-%20final.pdf

American Bar Association,
Resolution 112 (2019),
https://www.americanbar.org/co
ntent/dam/aba/administrative/ho
use_of_delegates/2019-annual-
supplemental-materials/112-
rev.pdf

American Bar Association,
Science & Technology Law
Section, *Report to the House of
Delegates Resolution 112* in
*Resolutions with Reports to the
House of Delegates* (2019),
https://www.americanbar.org/co

ntent/dam/aba/administrative/ho
use_of_delegates/ebook-of-
resolutions-with-reports/2019-
annual-electronic-resolution-
book.pdf

Aspen Institute, *Artificial
Intelligence and the Good
Society: The Search for New
Metrics, Governance, and a
Philosophical Perspective*
(2019),
http://csreports.aspeninstitute.or
g/documents/AI2019.pdf

Aspen Institute, *Artificial
Intelligence Comes of Age: The
Promise and Challenge of
Integrating AI into Cars,
Healthcare and Journalism*
(2017),
https://www.aspeninstitute.org/p
ublications/artificial-
intelligence-comes-age/

Aspen Institute, *Power Curve
Society: The Future of
Innovation, Opportunity and
Social Equity in the Emerging
Networked Economy* (2013),
https://assets.aspeninstitute.org/c
ontent/uploads/2013/02/Power-
Curve-Society.pdf

Arindrajit Basu, et. al, Center for
Internet and Society, India,
*Artificial Intelligence in the
Governance Sector in India*
(2018), https://cis-

india.org/internet-governance/ai-
and-governance-case-study-pdf

Berkman Klein Center, *Artificial
Intelligence & Human Rights:
Opportunities & Risks* (2018),
https://cyber.harvard.edu/sites/de
fault/files/2018-09/2018-
09_AIHumanRightsSmall.pdf

Brazil Ministry of Science,
Technology, Innovation and
Communications, Brazilian
Digital Transformation Strategy
E-Digital (2018),
http://www.mctic.gov.br/mctic/e
xport/sites/institucional/sessaoPu
blica/arquivos/digitalstrategy.pdf

British Embassy Mexico,
*Towards an AI Strategy in
Mexico: Harnessing the AI
Revolution* (2018),
http://go.wizeline.com/rs/571-
SRN-279/images/Towards-an-
AI-strategy-in-Mexico.pdf

Frederik Zuiderveen Borgesius,
Council of Europe,
*Discrimination, Artificial
Intelligence, and Algorithmic
Decision-Making* (2018),
https://rm.coe.int/discrimination-
artificial-intelligence-and-
algorithmic-decision-
making/1680925d73

J. Scott Brennen, Philip N.
Howard, & Rasmus Kleis
Nielsen, *An Industry-Led*

Debate: How UK Media Cover Artificial Intelligence (2018), https://reutersinstitute.politics.ox.ac.uk/sites/default/files/2018-

China, Standards Administration of China, *Artificial Intelligence Standardization White Paper (2018)*, https://baijiahao.baidu.com/s?id=1589996219403096393

China State Council, *Guideline on Next Generation AI Development Plan* (2017), http://www.gov.cn/zhengce/content/2017-07/20/content_5211996.htm

Centre for Data Ethics and Innovation, *Interim Report: Review into Bias in Algorithmic Decision-making* (2019), https://assets.publishing.service.gov.uk/government/uploads/system/uploads/attachment_data/file/819168/Interim_report_-_review_into_algorithmic_bias.pdf

CIFAR, *AICan2019: Annual Report of the CIFAR Pan-Canadian AI Strategy* (2019), https://www.cifar.ca/docs/default-source/ai-reports/ai_annualreport2019_web.pdf?sfvrsn=244ded44_17

Consultative Committee of the Convention for the Protection of Individuals with Regard to Automatic Processing of Personal Data (Convention 108), *Artificial Intelligence and Data Protection: Challenges and Possible Remedies* (2019), https://rm.coe.int/artificial-intelligence-and-data-protection-challenges-and-possible-re/168091f8a6

Consultative Committee of the Convention for the Protection of Individuals with Regard to Automatic Processing of Personal Data (Convention 108), *Guidelines on Artificial Intelligence and Data Protection (2019)*, https://rm.coe.int/guidelines-on-artificial-intelligence-and-data-protection/168091f9d8

Council of Europe, *A Study of the Implications of Advanced Digital Technologies (Including AI Systems) for the Concept of Responsibility Within a Human Rights Framework* (2019), https://rm.coe.int/a-study-of-the-implications-of-advanced-digital-technologies-including/168096bdab

Department for Digital Culture, Media & Sport, *UK Digital Strategy* (2017), https://www.gov.uk/government/publications/uk-digital-strategy/uk-digital-strategy

European Commission for the Efficiency of Justice, *European Ethical Charter on the Use of Artificial Intelligence in Judicial Systems and Their Environment* (2018), https://rm.coe.int/ethical-charter-en-for-publication-4-december-2018/16808f699c

Federal Government of Germany, *The National AI Strategy* (2018), https://www.ki-strategie-deutschland.de/home.html

France Strategie, *Intelligence artificielle et travail* (2018) https://www.strategie.gouv.fr/sites/strategie.gouv.fr/files/atoms/files/fs-rapport-intelligence-artificielle-28-mars-2018_0.pdf

Future Society, *The AIGO: A Framework for Planning, Developing, and Deploying Artificial Intelligence in Intergovernmental Organizations* (2018), http://thefuturesociety.org/wp-content/uploads/2019/08/AIGO_Report-vf.pdf

Future Society, *Governing the AI Adoption in Developing Countries* (2019), https://drive.google.com/file/d/1pdYNv9IZ0Aw6UsMOC_a5rqF4OH0wEIh2/view

Future World of Work, *Top 10 Principles for Ethical Artificial Intelligence* (2018) http://www.thefutureworldofwork.org/media/35420/uni_ethical_ai.pdf

G7, *Multistakeholder Exchange on Human Centric AI (Annex 2)* (2017), http://www.g8.utoronto.ca/ict/2017-ict-annex2-AI.html

G20, *Ministerial Statement on Trade and Digital Economy* (2019), https://g20tradedigital.go.jp/dl/Ministerial_Statement_on_Trade_and_Digital_Economy.pdf

Government digital Service & Office for Artificial Intelligence, UK, *A Guide to Using Artificial Intelligence in the Public Sector* (2019), https://www.gov.uk/government/collections/a-guide-to-using-artificial-intelligence-in-the-public-sector

Government of the Republic of Korea, *Mid- to Long-Term Master Plan in Preparation for the Intelligent Information Society* (2016), http://www.msip.go.kr/dynamic/file/afieldfile/msse56/1352869/2017/07/20/Master%20Plan%20for%20the%20intelligent%20information%20society.pdf

House of Lords, Select Committee on Artificial Intelligence, *AI in the UK: ready, willing and able?* (2018), https://publications.parliament.u k/pa/ld201719/ldselect/ldai/100/ 100.pdf 12/Brennen_UK_Media_Covera ge_of_AI_FINAL.pdf

IEEE, *Ethically Aligned Design, First Edition* (2019), https://ethicsinaction.ieee.org/

Internet Society, *Artificial Intelligence and Machine Learning: Policy Paper* (2017), https://www.internetsociety.org/r esources/doc/2017/artificial-intelligence-and-machine-learning-policy-paper/

ITI, *AI Policy Principles* (2017), https://www.itic.org/resources/A I-Policy-Principles-FullReport2.pdf

Japan Cabinet Office, Social Principles for Human Centric AI (2018), https://www8.cao.go.jp/cstp/stm ain/aisocialprinciples.pdf

Japan Strategic Council for AI Technology, *Report on Artificial Intelligence Technology Strategy* (2017), https://www.nedo.go.jp/content/ 100865202.pdf

Jeff Jonas & Ann Cavoukian, *Privacy by Design in the Age of Big Data* (2012), https://jeffjonas.typepad.com/Pri vacy-by-Design-in-the-Era-of-Big-Data.pdf

Mark Latonero, Data & Society, *Governing Artificial Intelligence: Upholding Human Rights & Dignity* (2018), https://datasociety.net/output/go verning-artificial-intelligence/

Law Society, *Algorithms in The Criminal Justice System* (2019), https://www.lawsociety.org.uk/s upport-services/research-trends/algorithm-use-in-the-criminal-justice-system-report/

Marten Kaevats, *Estonia's Ideas on Legalising AI* (2017), https://prezi.com/yabrlekhmcj4/ oecd-6-7min-paris/.

MSI-NET, Council of Europe, *Algorithms and Human Rights: Study on the Human Rights Dimensions of Automated Data Processing Techniques and Possible Regulatory Implications* (2017), https://rm.coe.int/algorithms-and-human-rights-study-on-the-human-rights-dimension-of-aut/1680796d10

National Science and Technology Council Committee on Technology, *Preparing for the Future of Artificial Intelligence* (2016), https://obamawhitehouse.archives.gov/sites/default/files/whitehouse_files/microsites/ostp/NSTC/preparing_for_the_future_of_ai.pdf

NIST, *U.S. Leadership in AI: A Plan for Federal Engagement in Developing Technical Standards and Related Tools* (2019), https://www.nist.gov/sites/default/files/documents/2019/08/10/ai_standards_fedengagement_plan_9aug2019.pdf

NITI Aayog, Government of India, *Discussion Paper: National Strategy for Artificial Intelligence #AIFORALL* (2018), https://www.niti.gov.in/writereaddata/files/document_publication/NationalStrategy-for-AI-Discussion-Paper.pdf

Nordic Council of Ministers, AI in the Nordic-Baltic region (2018), https://www.regeringen.se/49a602/globalassets/regeringen/dokument/naringsdepartementet/20180514_nmr_deklaration-slutlig-webb.pdf

OECD *Science Technology and Innovation Outlook 2018:* *Adapting to Technological and Societal Disruption* (2018), https://doi.org/10.1787/sti_in_outlook-2018-en

OECD, *Privacy Equity Investment in Artificial Intelligence* (2018), http://www.oecd.org/going-digital/ai/private-equity-investment-in-artificial-intelligence.pdf

Office of the Government of the Czech Republic, *Analysis of the Development Potential of Artificial Intelligence in the Czech Republic* (2018), https://www.vlada.cz/assets/evropske-zalezitosti/aktualne/AI-Summary-Report.pdf

Partnership on AI, *Report on Algorithmic Risk Assessment Tools in the U.S. Criminal Justice System* (2019), https://www.partnershiponai.org/wp-content/uploads/2019/04/Report-on-Algorithmic-Risk-Assessment-Tools.pdf

Personal Data Protection Commission Singapore, *Discussion Paper on Artificial Intelligence (AI) and Personal Data- Fostering Responsible Development and Adoption of AI* (2018), https://www.pdpc.gov.sg/-

/media/Files/PDPC/PDF-Files/Resource-for-Organisation/AI/Discussion-Paper-on-AI-and-PD---050618.pdf

Privacy International, *Privacy and Freedom of Expression In the Age of Artificial Intelligence* (2018), https://privacyinternational.org/report/1752/privacy-and-freedom-expression-age-artificial-intelligence

Privacy International, *Data is Power: Profiling and Automated Decision-Making in GDPR* (2017), https://privacyinternational.org/report/1718/data-power-profiling-and-automated-decision-making-gdpr

Robinson + Yu, *Civil Rights, Big Data, and Our Algorithmic Future* (2014), https://bigdata.fairness.io/wp-content/uploads/2014/09/Civil_Rights_Big_Data_and_Our_Algorithmic-Future_2014-09-12.pdf

Marc Rotenberg, *Algorithmic Transparency and Emerging Privacy Issues*, UNESCO Presentation (2015), https://epic.org/2015/UNESCO-AlgorTransparency.pdf

Royal Society, *Machine Learning: The Power and Promise of Computers That Learn by Example* (2017), https://royalsociety.org/-/media/policy/projects/machine-learning/publications/machine-learning-report.pdf

Russian President Vladimir Putin, *Artificial Intelligence Technology Development Meeting* (2019), http://kremlin.ru/events/president/news/page/14

Select Committee on Artificial Intelligence, *National Artificial Intelligence Research and Development Strategic Plan: 2019 Update* (2019), https://www.whitehouse.gov/wpcontent/uploads/2019/06/National-AI-Research-and-Development-Strategic-Plan-2019-UpdateJune-2019.pdf

Singapore Infocomm Media Development Authority, *Digital Economy Framework for Action* (2018), https://www.imda.gov.sg/-/media/imda/files/sg-digital/sgd-framework-for-action.pdf?la=en

Darrell M. West & John R. Allen, Brookings Institution, *How Artificial Intelligence Is Transforming the World* (2018), https://www.brookings.edu/resea

rch/how-artificial-intelligence-is-transforming-the-world/

UK Information Commissioner's Office, *Big Data, Artificial Intelligence, Machine Learning and Data Protection* (2017), https://ico.org.uk/media/for-organisations/documents/201355 9/big-data-ai-ml-and-data-protection.pdf

World Government Summit, Summary Report 2018: Global Governance AI Roundtable (2018), https://www.worldgovernmentsu mmit.org/api/publications/docu ment?id=ff6c88c5-e97c-6578-b2f8-ff0000a7ddb6

Articles

Hunt Allcott & Matthew Gentzkow, *Social Media and Fake News in the 2016 Election*, Journal of Economic Perspectives (2017)

Jack Balkin, *The Three Laws of Robotics in the Age of Big Data*, Ohio State Law Journal (2017)

Solon Barocas & Andrew D. Selbst, *Big Data's Disparate Impact*, California Law Review (2016)

Miriam C Buiten, *Towards Intelligent Regulation of Artificial Intelligence*, Cambridge University Press (2019)

Ryan Calo, *Robots and Privacy*, in *Robot Ethics: The Ethical and Social Implications of Robotics* (2012)

Ryan Calo, *Artificial Intelligence Policy: A Primer and Roadmap*, University of California Davis (2017)

Anupam Chander, *The Racist Algorithm?*, Michigan Law Review (2017)

Danielle Citron & Frank Pasquale, *The Scored Society: Due Process for Automated Predictions*, Washington Law Review (2014)

Danielle Keats Citron, *Technological Due Process*, Washington University Law Review (2008)

Corinne Cath, *Governing Artificial Intelligence: Ethical, Legal and Technical Opportunities and Challenges*, Philosophical Transactions. Series A, Mathematical, Physical, and Engineering Sciences (2018)

Cary Coglianese & David Lehr, *Transparency and Algorithmic Governance*, Administrative Law Review (2018)

Julie E. Cohen, *Power/play: Discussion of Configuring the Networked Self*, Jerusalem Review of Legal Studies (2012)

Angele Christin, Alex Rosenblat, & Danah Boyd, *Courts and Predictive Algorithms*, Data & Civil Rights (2015)

Kate Crawford, *The Hidden Biases of Big Data*, Harvard Business Review (2013)

Rebecca Crootof, *The Killer Robots Are Here: Legal and Policy Implications*, Cardozo Law Review (2015)

Daniel Dennett, *When HAL kills, who's to blame?*, in *Rethinking Responsibility in Science and Technology* (2014)

Nicholas Diakopoulos, *Algorithmic Accountability: journalistic Investigation of Computational Power Structures*, Digital Journalism (2015)

Cynthia Dwork & Aaron Roth, *The Algorithmic Foundations of Differential Privacy*, Theoretical Computer Science (2014)

Batya Friedman & Helen Nissenbaum, *Bias in Computer Systems*, ACM Transactions on Information Systems (1996)

Bryce Goodman & Seth Flaxman, *European Union Regulations on Algorithmic Decision Making and a "Right to Explanation,"* AI Magazine (2017)

Iria Giuffrida, Fredric Lederer, & Nicolas Vermerys, *A Legal Perspective on the Trials and Tribulations of AI: How Artificial Intelligence, the Internet of Things, Smart Contracts, and Other Technologies Will Affect the Law*, Case Western Reserve Law (2018)

Aziz Z. Huq, *Racial Equity in Algorithmic Criminal Justice* Duke Law Journal (2019)

Anna Jobin, Marcello Ienca, & Effy Vayena, *The Global Landscape of Ai Ethics Guidelines*, Nature (2019)

Sonia K Katyal, *Private Accountability in the Age of Artificial Intelligence*, UCLA Law Review (2019)

Danielle Kehl, Priscilla Guo, Samuel Kessler, *Algorithms in the Criminal Justice System: Assessing the Use of Risk Assessments in Sentencing*, Harvard (2017)

Ian Kerr & Jessica Earle, *Prediction, Preemption, Presumption, How Big Data Threatens Big Picture Privacy*, Stanford Law Review Online (2013)

Lauren Kirchner, Julia Angwin, Jeff Larson & Surya Mattu, *Machine Bias: There's Software Used Across the Country to Predict Future Criminals. And It's Biased Against Blacks*, ProPublica (2016)

Joshua A. Kroll, Solon Barocas, Edward W. Felten, Joel R. Reidenberg; David G. Robinson; Harlan Yu, *Accountable Algorithms*, University of Pennsylvania Law Review (2017)

Paul B. de Laat, *Big data and algorithmic decision-making: can transparency restore accountability?*, ACM SIGCAS Computers and Society (2017)

Alessandro Mantelero, *AI and Big Data: A Blueprint for a Human Rights, Social and Ethical Impact Assessment*,

Computer Law and Security Review (2018)

Frank Pasquale, *Restoring Transparency to Automated Authority*, Journal on Telecommunications and High Tech Law (2011)

Dawinder S. Sidhu, *Moneyball Sentencing*, Boston College Law Review (2015)

Ric Simmons, *Big Data, Machine Judges, and the Legitimacy of the Criminal Justice System*, University of California Davis (2018)

Robert H. Sloan & Richard Warner, *When Is an Algorithm Transparent?: Predictive Analytics, Privacy, and Public Policy*, IEEE: Security & Privacy (2018)

Samuel C. Woolley & Douglas R. Guilbeault, Computational Propaganda in the United States of America: Manufacturing Consensus Online, Oxford (2017)

Cedric Villani, AI for Humanity, *For a Meaningful Artificial Intelligence - Towards a French and European Strategy* (2018), https://www.aiforhumanity.fr/pdfs/9782111457089_Rapport_Villani_accessible.pdf

Vinnova, *Artificial Intelligence in Swedish Business and Society* (2018), https://www.vinnova.se/contentassets/29cd313d690e4be3a8d861ad05a4ee48/vr_18_09.pdf

Tal Z. Zarsky, *Understanding Discrimination in the Scored Society*, Washington Law Review (2014)

Jonathan L. Zittrain, *Engineering an Election*, Harvard Law Review Forum (2014)

Books

Ajay Agrawal, Joshua Gans, Avi Goldfarb, *Prediction Machines: The Simple Economics of Artificial Intelligence* (2018)

James Barratt, *Our Final Invention: Artificial Intelligence and the End of the Human Era* (2015)

Nick Bostrom, *Superintelligence: Paths, Dangers, Strategies* (2014)

Ryan Calo, A. Michael Froomkin, & Ian Kerr, *Robot Law* (2016)

Brian Christian & Tom Griffiths, *Algorithms to Live By: The Computer Science of Human Decisions* (2016)

Paul Daugherty & H. James Wilson, *Human + Machine: Reimagining Work in the Age of AI* (2018)

Pedro Domingos, *The Master Algorithm: How the Quest for the Ultimate Learning Machine Will Remake Our World* (2018)

Cynthia Dwork, *The Algorithmic Foundations of Differential Privacy* (2014)

Virginia Eubanks, *Automating Inequality: How High-Tech Tools Profile, Police, and Punish the Poor* (2018)

Martin Ford, *Rise of the Robots: Technology and the Threat of a Jobless Future* (2015)

Yuval Noah Harari, *Homo Deus: A Brief History of Tomorrow* (2017)

Gary Kasparov, *Deep Thinking* (2017)

Kai-Fu Lee, *AI Super-Powers: China, Silicon Valley, and the New World Order* (2018)

Safiya Umoja Noble, *Algorithms of Oppression: How Search Engines Reinforce Racism* (2018)

Cathy O'Neil, *Weapons of Math Destruction* (2016)

OECD, *Artificial Intelligence In Society* (2019)

Frank Pasquale, *The Black Box Society: The Secret Algorithms That Control Money and Information* (2015)

Krish Schaffer, *Data versus Democracy: How Big Data Algorithms Shape Opinions and Alter the Course of History* (2019)

Paul Scharre, *Army of None: Autonomous Weapons and the Future of War* (2019)

Christopher Steiner, *Automate This: How Algorithms Came to Rule Our World* (2012)

Max Tegmark, *Life 3.0: Being Human in the Age of Artificial Intelligence* (2018)

Eric Tropol, *Deep Medicine: How Artificial Intelligence Can Make Healthcare Human Again* (2019)

Joseph Weizenbaum, *Computer Power and Human Reason: From Judgment to Calculation* (1976)

Norbert Wiener, *The Human Use Of Human Beings: Cybernetics And Society (The Da Capo Series in Science)* (1988)

Made in the
USA
Middletown, DE